Praise for *What to Ask the Person in the Mirror*

"Drawing on years of experience in business and academia, Rob Kaplan has produced a very readable book that provides unique and valuable insights into management, including what makes and sustains highly successful leaders. Read this wonderful book if you want to understand how great managers grow and mature, navigate pitfalls, and bounce back from adversity."

—Dr. Mohamed A. El-Erian, CEO, PIMCO;
author, *When Markets Collide*

"Rob Kaplan's book is my new leadership bible. His extensive experience leading others and his time coaching great leaders has given him a unique understanding of what breeds success and failure. Leaders from any type of business can benefit from Kaplan's guidance."

—Caryn Seidman-Becker, CEO, CLEAR Corporation

"For someone like me who is building a business and growing an entrepreneurial company, this book becomes the road map and go-to guide for asking the really tough questions that ultimately allow the truly successful business leader to emerge."

—Tyra Banks, supermodel turned entrepreneur

WHAT
TO ASK
THE PERSON
IN THE
MIRROR

WHAT
TO ASK
THE PERSON
IN THE
MIRROR

Critical Questions for Becoming a More Effective
Leader and Reaching Your Potential

ROBERT STEVEN KAPLAN

Harvard Business Review Press

Boston, Massachusetts

No part of this publication may be reproduced, stored in or introduced into a retrieval system, or transmitted, in any form, or by any means (electronic, mechanical, photocopying, recording, or otherwise), without the prior permission of the publisher. Requests for permission should be directed to permissions@hbsp.harvard.edu, or mailed to Permissions, Harvard Business School Publishing, 60 Harvard Way, Boston, Massachusetts 02163.

Library of Congress Cataloging-in-Publication Data

Kaplan, Robert S.
    What to ask the person in the mirror : critical questions for becoming a more effective leader and reaching your potential / Robert S. Kaplan.
        p. cm.
    ISBN 978-1-4221-7001-4 (alk. paper)
    1. Leadership. 2. Executive ability. I. Title.
    HD57.7.K3663 2011
    658.4'092—dc22

                                2011008441

The paper used in this publication meets the requirements of the American National Standard for Permanence of Paper for Publications and Documents in Libraries and Archives Z39.48-1992.

To my parents, who taught me to never stop asking questions, and to all those who over the generations have protected our right to do so.

Contents

Introduction

Great leadership is not about having all the answers—
it is, more often, about having the courage to
ask the critical questions

> **How do you go about improving your ability to be a**
> **more outstanding executive and leader?**
>
> **Is this something you can learn?**
>
> **Can leadership skills be taught?**
>
> **Are excellent leaders made or born?**
>
> **How do the great ones do it?**

Many people believe that great leaders are just blessed with a knack for having the right answers. They believe that these people have a natural instinct for knowing what to do in any given situation—how to stay on track, inspire employees to work toward a common goal, organize effectively, and drive their businesses. Superb leaders, they suspect, are born with certain talents, insight, and charisma that make them different from the rest of us. Of course, these excellent leaders are very *sure* of themselves—because it comes so *naturally* to them!

It is a pretty common notion: there is a rarified species of successful leaders who follow an orderly path upward during their careers, consistently avoid significant setbacks, do not suffer periods of confusion, seldom feel like failures, and have an uncanny knack for looking around corners and seeing into the future.

Sounds nice, but I don't think so.

Over the past twenty-five years—first as a business executive and then as a professor of management practice at Harvard Business School—I have led several businesses and regularly advised a wide variety of senior executives and emerging leaders. I have certainly made my share of mistakes and, from them, gained greater insight into leadership approaches that tend to enhance executive effectiveness as well as those practices that often undermine performance.

In the course of these experiences, I have found that *almost without exception*, successful leaders go through significant periods of time in which they feel confused, discouraged, and unsure of themselves and their decisions. They feel as if they should be somewhere else, doing something else. They wonder why other executives seem to have an easier time doing *their* jobs. They go through wrenching phases in which they grasp for answers and feel fundamentally alone. Even as they project an air of confidence, they harbor deep feelings of uncertainty and apprehension.

Many successful executives find it hard to believe that other successful peers are feeling this way. "If that's true," they often ask me skeptically, "then what's the difference between successful executives and those who are less successful?"

My answer: a key difference between those who reach their potential and those who don't is *how they deal with these periods of confusion and uncertainty*. The trick lies not in avoiding these difficult periods; it lies in knowing how to step back, diagnose, regroup, and move forward.

Lonely at the Top

Of course, this is far easier to describe than to accomplish. As executives become more senior—perhaps ultimately becoming chief executive of their organizations—it becomes far more difficult to get timely and constructive feedback, maintain an accurate self-perception, and develop early warning systems for emerging problems. At this point in your career, you have fewer (if any) superiors closely observing your behavior. As a result, the first time you're likely to hear a critique of your performance is during your year-end review with your boss—or, if you're CEO, with your board of directors—or perhaps when your business experiences a visible setback. By that time, unfortunately, it may be too late to take the kinds of corrective actions that could prevent permanent damage to your business, or to your career.

The phrase *lonely at the top* is overused. It's a succinct and accurate way, though, to capture the dilemma I am describing.

I have certainly experienced this difficult dilemma myself and also observed it in other executives over the course of my career and, particularly, since coming to Harvard. As a result of these experiences—I have come to believe that, for most leaders, 90 percent of the battle is being able to step back and take the time to *ask the right questions*—questions that help you figure out how to gain insight, regroup, and move forward.

Asking the Critical Questions

Let me stress, again, that successful business leaders seldom have all the answers. Instead, they are very good at knowing how and when to *ask the critical questions* that help them frame issues, diagnose problems, and develop action plans—both for their companies and for themselves. In this way, these executives are able to work through adversity and get themselves and their companies back on track.

In this book, I share my experiences in helping executives step back, diagnose their situations, and successfully move ahead. I have worked with numerous executives to develop and then internalize this mind-set, so that they ultimately "own" a tailored approach to inquiry that they continue to practice into the future, long after I've left the scene.

Creating a menu of potential inquiry, and creating a process whereby key questions can be framed and debated, is a big part of what this book is about. I strongly believe that executives need to pursue this approach in ways that are tailored to themselves and their stage of career, and also fit the particular needs of their industries and organizations. In the chapters that follow, I will provide numerous examples of how executives in a variety of contexts have gone about framing key questions, and creating a process to address those challenges effectively.

The central premise of this book is that by knowing how and when to ask critical questions, a young professional as well as a senior leader can take greater ownership of his or her organization and career. Asking the right questions, in ways that frame key issues cogently, is far more important than having all the answers. In fact, in my experience, if a leader asks the right questions and is open to a path of true inquiry, compelling insights tend to "fall out" as a matter of course. How many times has someone asked you a well-framed question that causes a lightbulb to go off in your head? Sometimes just hearing and then thinking about the right question opens your mind, and steers you in a new and constructive direction.

The challenge, therefore, is twofold: framing the right questions, and getting in the habit of regularly stepping back and asking them.

What to Ask the Person in the Mirror

I have distilled this approach down to seven basic types of inquiry that—in my experience—resonate with both business and nonprofit leaders. In each of the following chapters, I present one of these sets of key questions, and discuss different approaches to framing them and then answering them.

Despite how firmly you may believe you know yourself and your organization, you may well find that it requires a surprising amount of additional inquiry and reflection to adequately address these issues. In addition, I think you'll find that these questions tend to build on one another—in other words, addressing the first sets of questions should make it much easier for you to attack subsequent questions.

The areas of focus, in sequence, are as follows:

Vision and priorities. This is the foundation of your enterprise. It is critical to have a clearly articulated vision and accompanying key priorities that are widely understood throughout your organization and by key constituencies. When a business is struggling, the problem often grows out of confusion regarding the vision and associated priorities. In this chapter, we will discuss vision—its importance, and how you might formulate or reformulate your vision. In addition, we will break down various aspects of how to identify a manageable list of priorities, which, in turn, will help you achieve your goals and aspirations.

Managing your time. Do you know how you spend your time? Does it match your vision and key priorities? Often, well-intentioned leaders are not fully aware of the severe cost of a mismatch between how they spend their time and their top priorities. This chapter will address this mismatch and its costs, and suggest specific ways to ensure that you actually spend your time, with a more laserlike focus, on your most important priorities.

Giving and getting feedback. Once you've established a clear vision and priorities, effective coaching is a critical tool for achieving these objectives. While most leaders understand this, many still don't effectively coach their subordinates in order to ensure outstanding performance. In addition, many leaders fail to get the critical coaching that they themselves need in order to excel. In this chapter, I will discuss several pitfalls and misconceptions regarding talent management. We will also explore other critical issues and review several alternative approaches relating to coaching and being coached.

Succession planning and delegation. Do you have a nucleus of talent that you are focused on developing? Are you deploying, coaching, and adding to that talent base in a manner that builds your enterprise? Are you consciously delegating key tasks to these professionals? This part of the book will address several central questions that leaders should ask in order to build and develop their human capital. We also discuss the critical importance of delegating certain tasks so that you have the bandwidth to focus your time on the most critical priorities of the enterprise.

Evaluation and alignment. Does the design of your enterprise and your approach to leading still fit the needs of the business? Are you pursuing practices that worked at one time but urgently need to be updated, revised, or scrapped? How do you create the processes, emotional distance, and bandwidth to address these questions? We will address several of the toughest issues that leaders must face, and effectively deal with, if they are to achieve sustained success.

The leader as role model. Your actions speak louder than your words. Are you fully aware of the messages you and your direct reports are sending with your behaviors? Do you and your subordinates say one thing but contradict those messages by doing another? Many emerging leaders, and even some senior executives, fail to appreciate the impact of their actions on their subordinates and key constituencies. We will explore what it really means to be a role model, and discuss the important questions leaders must address in order to be effective role models in their organizations.

Reaching your potential. Do you know your own strengths, weaknesses, and passions? Do you foster a learning environment in which your subordinates can reach their potential? Do you encourage candid debate, and work to create a culture in which justice and fairness prevail in your organization? If not, how are these drawbacks negatively affecting your firm and its performance? This chapter will explore how you can take ownership of knowing yourself, manage yourself in a manner that brings out your best, and create this mind-set among your subordinates. I will suggest several specific techniques for making progress on these important matters.

As you read each chapter, you will see that this approach is intended, first, to help you gain real insight into yourself and your organization. Longer term, and more important, it is intended to get you started on the path of regular inquiry: framing issues in productive ways, stepping back to gain insights, and then *acting* on those insights in order to successfully move forward. The final chapter of this book will talk about ways to make this approach a regular part of your leadership activities.

The Practice of Inquiry and Reflection

Several of the questions and approaches in this book are likely to strike a chord with you. Depending on your situation and experiences, others may not. On the basis of your preferences and leadership style, you might even develop a number of questions that speak to you more deeply than the ones in this book. The important thing is that you get into the habit of identifying a set of questions that fit your organization and industry, suit your personality and personal profile, and sync up with the reality of your situation. As you try this approach, I hope that you see it as a valuable tool—useful when you're feeling uncertain, or as a preemptive course check as you build your skill set, your career, and your company.

My goal is to get you started on this path. I hope this mindset will allow you to better navigate the challenging and rewarding journey of becoming a more effective manager, and a truly outstanding leader.

1

Vision and Priorities

If You Know Where You're Going,
It's a Lot Easier to Get There

Have you developed a clear vision for your enterprise?

Have you identified three to five key priorities to achieve that vision?

Do you actively communicate this vision, and associated key priorities, to your organization?

In order to understand a business or nonprofit—and assess the challenges facing its leader—it is critically important to begin with the question "What is your vision for this enterprise?" What do you hope to achieve in the years ahead? What is special about this organization? Why do you spend your precious time working at this firm? Can you communicate the vision clearly and effectively, so that it is well understood by your employees and key stakeholders?

In my experience, almost every sustained success enjoyed by an effective leader and his or her organization derives from a clearly articulated vision. A clear vision mobilizes your employees and communicates where you want to take the enterprise. It can create the motivation that your people need to get out of bed in the morning, come to work, and give it their best! Taking the time to carefully develop your vision—an *aspiration* for your enterprise—is critical to creating the foundation for building an outstanding business or nonprofit organization. As Yogi Berra is reputed to have said, "If you know where you're going, it's a lot easier to get there."

In business, where your time and other resources are scarce, you and your people had better know where you're going before making critical decisions. In this chapter, we will explore the critical importance of vision, review several specific examples, and discuss how a vision can be formulated and developed to provide a compelling beacon for your organization.

Vision alone is not enough—it must be accompanied by the identification of a manageable number of key priorities. These priorities specify the critical tasks that must be accomplished in order to achieve the vision. I will suggest various approaches to defining these top priorities, making necessary trade-off decisions, and updating those choices on a regular basis.

A vision and its associated priorities must be actively communicated. This chapter will address the importance of effective communication—and over-communication!—of your vision and priorities so that your employees and other important stakeholders clearly understand where you're heading, and where you want them to focus in order to achieve organizational objectives.

Your vision and priorities should be adaptable and dynamic. Throughout this chapter, we will discuss the need to adapt the overall vision and priorities to your specific regions and business units, as well as the need to update the vision and crucial priorities to fit the continuing challenges of a changing world.

What Is a Vision?

A vision is a clear articulation of what you would like your enterprise to be if you succeed.[1] When you look back five years from now, what would you like to be able to say that you've accomplished? What is your dream for this organization?

For starters, a vision should be fundamentally based on a careful analysis and identification of your distinctive competencies. What are you truly great at? How are you differentiated from your competitors?

The newly appointed CEO of a business that specialized in office products distribution was looking for ways to get off to a good start as she began her new role. The business had been in her family for three generations and was 100 percent owned by family members. When we first met, I asked about her vision for the business. "Well, the office products business is a bit bland," she explained. "It doesn't really lend itself to visions and aspirations."

"Well, it *does* sound like a commodity business," I responded. "So how do you differentiate yourself? Why would I buy office products from you versus someone else? What do you hope to achieve in this business?"

She had a ready response: "First, we only sell to businesses and institutions, not individuals. We have a number of long-term relationships focused on the northeastern United States.

We pride ourselves on offering a full product line, so that our customers can use us as their one-stop source. We're not the lowest-price option, but we are distinctive in terms of breadth of product offering, outstanding service, our ability to do rush orders—even if they're uneconomic, at times—and our willingness to source unusual or custom requests. We take a lot of pride in being an indispensable backbone supplier of office products to our customers."

What did her answer demonstrate? Over the decades, company leadership had made fundamental choices that defined this enterprise in a distinctive way. The company was designed to deliver on a well-defined value proposition, and this CEO and her colleagues were working hard to achieve that vision today. They took enormous pride in a job well done.

After additional discussion about the future direction of the business, she concluded that it would be valuable to reexamine, update, and rearticulate the vision. This was particularly timely given the fact that many of the company's employees had been with the firm for less than three years. In addition, several recent changes in the competitive landscape, if left unanswered, might threaten the sustainability of several of the company's distinctive competencies. She wanted to make sure that her employees were on the "same page" regarding where they were heading and what she wanted the company to achieve.

More Than Just Money

Employees, partners, and other constituents need an aspiration if they are to do and be their best. While it's true that money can be a great motivator for a while, I've observed that people eventually get burned out and lose their passion if money is their primary driver. The fact is, they need something more. They need something bigger than themselves to strive for. This may be building a great business, making a positive impact on the world, or simply contributing to an organization that is the very best at something.

Human beings are social animals. They want to belong. They want to be part of an organization that has meaning— and, by extension, helps give their lives meaning. Why do highly talented people, with a multitude of attractive career options, become federal prosecutors for relatively low compensation? Why do others choose to teach school? Why do still others join the military and put their lives on the line? The answer is compelling: they aspire to something that is bigger and more meaningful than financial reward.

People want to be proud of what they do. Yes, they want to be rewarded, but they typically need other reasons to "join up" and stay with an organization. Otherwise, they'll treat it as a convenient stopping point on the way to something more meaningful.

A clearly articulated aspiration gives you and your employees a reason to spring out of bed in the morning and—very often—go the extra mile. *Achieving* that aspiration gives people a deep kind of satisfaction, which serves as reinforcement in a number of important realms.

What role does money play? Money is a by-product of successfully achieving the vision. It creates incentives for the type of behaviors you want to encourage. If you do a superb job, money will follow. This is sometimes referred to as *long-term greedy*. Great organizations understand the pitfalls of taking the kinds of actions that generate near-term profits but undermine the reputation, character, and aspiration of the enterprise. On the other hand, they also understand that, in some cases, trade-offs need to be made in order to help build the franchise. For example, making a concession to a key customer who needs help is likely to sacrifice near-term profits, but it may very well help solidify a long-term relationship that is critical to building the franchise—leading to greater long-term profits and help-ing to realize the vision.

Putting It into Practice: The Prism

A clear vision makes trade-off decisions much clearer. It con-veys your reason for being. It shapes and influences every key decision that you make. It outlines what you will do, and what you won't do. It is the essential prism through which signifi-cant decisions should be made.

More specifically, it guides you (and your people) in deter-mining which customers you will serve, what types of prod-ucts/services to offer, whom you should hire, how you should organize and compensate, what type of culture you need to build, and what kinds of leadership styles you should embrace. Establishing this vision helps you make each of these critical decisions, and focuses your employees on striving to accom-plish your major goals.

If you carefully observe great organizations, large and small, you'll notice that they are organized around a clear vision. You'll see the CEO and other key leaders confidently explain-ing what they will do and won't do—and why they make certain critical decisions the way they do. You will see confidence and passion in these explanations.

You will see similar confidence, passion, and pride among their people. Their actions are guided by this vision. Typically, their success—and, as mentioned earlier, the profits that they generate—are a by-product of striving to achieve this vision.

Conversely, in enterprises that are off track, you will often see confusion and uncertainty about the vision. They may have previously had a coherent set of aspirations, but due to poor leadership, changes in the environment, or other factors, they are no longer confident about where they're heading and what they're supposed to do. They wrestle with questions like these:

- Are we in business to serve clients with a particular set of high-value-added products, or is our primary goal to generate profits—even if that outcome is not in the best interests or our clients/customers?

- Do we still believe in innovation and new product development, or do quarterly profit pressures mean we need to suspend or deemphasize this effort?

- Has the pressure to generate profits overridden a previously broadly understood vision about values and serving our customers and communities?

It's my experience that when organizations are off track, they will stay confused until their leadership—sometimes spurred by an astute board of directors—pushes for a rearticulation of a clear vision, based on distinctive competencies and core values.

What's needed, in other words, is a compelling restatement of "who we are and where we're going."

Examples of the Power of a Clear Vision

A clear vision is powerful. It mobilizes large groups of people. It inspires and motivates them, and it gives them clear direction. Let's look at some examples.

"I Have a Dream": Advancing Civil Rights

Martin Luther King, Jr. gave his most famous speech on the steps of the Lincoln Memorial on August 28, 1963. At Harvard, we often use this speech to demonstrate the power of a clearly articulated vision. King's masterful piece of oratory is remembered today as the "I have a dream" speech, because he began several powerful paragraphs with that four-word phrase:

> *I have a dream that one day on the red hills of Georgia the sons of former slaves and the sons of former slave owners will be able to sit down together at a table of brotherhood.*
>
> *I have a dream that one day even the state of Mississippi, a desert state, sweltering with the heat of injustice and oppression, will be transformed into an oasis of freedom and justice.*
>
> *I have a dream that my four children will one day live in a nation where they will not be judged by the color of their skin but by the content of their character.*[2]

A brilliant vision, brilliantly delivered. Other parts of the vision are not so often remembered but were nevertheless integral. "We must not allow our creative protest to degenerate into physical violence," King cautioned. He also made clear that the movement would need to develop alliances with white people and other various key constituencies: "We cannot walk alone." At the same time, he stressed that while such alliances were critical, they had to support the vision: "We must make the pledge that we shall march ahead . . . We cannot turn back."

This vision was repeated countless times by King in numerous speeches he gave throughout the country. It also was translated by his key lieutenants and followers into specific initiatives and priorities: a subject that we will return to shortly. The ultimate result was something unthinkable at the time: the passage of the Civil Rights Act of 1964, and a fundamental change in the rights of minorities in the United States.

Curing Spinal Cord Injury: Creating a Center of Excellence in Spinal Cord Injury Research

The Miami Project to Cure Paralysis was started in 1984 with a vision to "cure spinal cord injury." At that time, very little research was being done on spinal cord injury, and the articulation of such a bold vision was considered audacious—even imprudent. The project's founder, Nick Buoniconti, believed that he needed to lay out an audacious vision in order to galvanize potential followers into taking action. In effect, he dared them to dream about seeing patients walk again. He repeated the vision in each of his speeches and included it in every Miami Project mailing.

This vision *did* help mobilize families of victims and potential donors. Twenty-five years later, The Miami Project has raised more than $300 million, has pioneered critical breakthroughs in treating spinal cord injury, and today is actively working on a number of promising treatments. All of this progress would have seemed impossible a decade or two ago.

It is true that a cure for spinal cord injuries still remains a dream, and—given the boldness of the vision—this has created some angst for the organization. The relative infrequency of these kinds of injuries renders them "orphans," in the sense that academic and pharmaceutical researchers aren't as inclined to heavily invest in groundbreaking research because the market for effective treatments is likely to remain small. Nevertheless, The Miami Project leadership found that a clear and bold aspiration was and is essential, to help mobilize the various key constituents in order to make substantive progress.[3]

To the World Series: The Quest to Be the Best!

The founder of the Kansas City Royals, Ewing Kauffman, articulated a vision for the team at its inception in 1969. He promised that within five years, Kansas City would have such an outstanding team that it would compete in a World Series. He repeated this vision in every speech he gave to fans, players, employees, and other constituents, as well as in his numerous radio and television interviews.

This vision seemed more than a bit unrealistic to most observers. After all, this was a baseball town that hadn't had a major league team for several years. There were few name players at the start, there were only the beginnings of a minor league farm system, and—by the standards of the bigger clubs in major metropolitan cities—Kansas City was a relatively small market.

Despite this, Kauffman was undaunted in emphasizing his aspiration. He repeated the vision frequently and consistently over several years. This vision guided every action he and the organization took. He insisted on excellence in every key aspect of the organization. Critical decisions that he and his organization made always had to pass a demanding test: were they consistent with achieving the vision of being the *best*? Player acquisitions, farm system design, facilities, general manager selection, and coaching choices—all had to pass through this prism.

While there wasn't a World Series in Kansas City within five years, there was one within ten years, and—in 1985—the team won the World Series. It's fair to say that this would never have been accomplished without the clear, compelling vision articulated by Ewing Kauffman.

One America: Unifying the Country to Address Our Major Challenges

A relatively unknown politician from Illinois delivered the keynote speech at the 2004 Democratic National Convention. In that speech, Barack Obama articulated a vision for the country: "There is not a liberal America and a conservative America—there is the United States of America. There is not a Black America and a White America and Latino America and Asian America, there's the United States of America."[4]

It was a vision of unification—a depiction of a nation coming together to resolve the major issues that faced it. The power of Obama's oratory transformed him into a national figure. He repeated the vision on a regular basis. Between 2006 and 2008, he built on the support that his vision had generated to mobilize a huge campaign organization, assemble a senior policy team, and develop an enormous donor base. On the basis of this effort, he ultimately won the Democratic nomination and then the presidency in 2008. His powerful vision was central to the organization and mobilization of this successful campaign.

A Vision of Access: Creating Opportunity for Outstanding, but Economically Challenged, Students

In 1997, the TEAK Fellowship was established, based on the vision that outstanding but economically disadvantaged New York City junior high school students should have the same access to superb high school choices as their more economically advantaged peers.[5]

The organization then developed a detailed road map for how this vision would be accomplished. It worked closely with parents and potential fellows to develop effective admission and financial aid procedures. It accepted twenty fellows per year, based on intensive screening and interview processes. It helped develop intensive tutoring programs in math, English, music, and other subjects that it deemed to be essential to student development.

Thanks to its clearly articulated vision and plans, TEAK was able to attract staff, donors, a strong board of directors, and—most important—highly qualified students. Thirteen years later, it has produced more than 300 fellows who have graduated from many of the finest high schools and colleges in the United States.

Even at the Corner Diner, There Is a Vision

I've deliberately chosen a range of contexts to illustrate the concept of vision in the fields of politics and nonprofits. It's not different in the field of business. Great *enterprises*, broadly defined, are based on a clear vision. In fact, it's hard to think of an example of a successful business that *doesn't* have one. This vision is likely to have evolved over time, but it is there, guiding the firm into the future.

There is a diner on the corner of my street in New York City—a modest establishment that has been my favorite place to eat for the past fifteen years. The owner founded the restaurant more than thirty years ago. His vision was to build a friendly neighborhood restaurant that provided basic food (hamburgers, chicken, soups, salads, basic breakfasts, and good coffee) at a fair price, with prompt service and very modest decor in a convenient location. Every key decision the owner and his colleagues make today is still consistent with this vision: minimal staff, no credit cards (to save on fees), a large counter for walk-ins, and so on.

Again: the diner's success emanates from the vision that lies behind it. They may not think consciously in these terms, but their operation certainly embodies the concept of *vision*.

Developing a Vision: Some Useful Exercises

If you agree that the articulation of a clear vision is important, how do you go about developing such a vision? I have worked with numerous leaders and their senior management teams, in for-profit as well as nonprofit settings, to achieve that important goal. Usually, a strong aspiration is lurking in the background and minds of most leaders and their senior staff. The trick is to identify it, give it voice, and ultimately, write it down.

I find it is often useful to do a few exercises to help people loosen up, shake off the cobwebs, and focus. For example,

I normally ask some of the following questions (and, standing at a blackboard or whiteboard, I write down what I hear in response):

- Why do you work at this organization? You could work elsewhere; why do you work *here*? What do you love about this organization?

- What would you like to tell your grandchildren about why you worked at this place for thirty years of your life? Again, you could have worked elsewhere; how will you explain why you chose here? To what great cause/ accomplishment has this organization contributed?

- What would you like this enterprise to look like in ten years? What would you hope to say that it accomplished?

- What are the distinctive competencies of this organization? What would the world lose, or forgo, if it didn't exist?

When confronted with questions like these, people generally let their imaginations run free and allow their dreams come to the fore. This exercise is done most effectively in groups of senior executives (including the CEO) in a relaxed atmosphere, where each participant is expected to speak, and no one person is allowed to dominate the conversation.

Why Did We Wait So Long to Talk About This?

In my experience, putting longtime colleagues in a position where they can listen to each other is surprisingly illuminating to those in the room. It often helps them understand, in many cases for the first time, why they have been at loggerheads for months or years over certain key decisions: they were unaware that they each had visions for the organization that were somewhat at odds with those of their colleagues. Typically, they make comments along the lines of, "Now I understand why you've been so stubborn in pushing for initiative X or action Y! Now I get it. If I had understood your motivation earlier, I think I probably would have agreed with you, rather than disagreeing with you all this time."

In many cases, these visioning sessions help colleagues gain a new understanding of, and a new respect for, each other. It also forces these executives to challenge each other and refocus on true core competencies. Some of those core competencies may have evolved over time. The world may have changed, so that certain competitive advantages have eroded, while others have been built. Does the vision still reflect their core competencies today? This discussion often requires quite a bit of homework (in preparation), soul-searching, and updated macro and competitive analysis.

I encourage organizations to do this exercise at least once a year. In periods of change and increased uncertainty (particularly brought about by changes in the external environment), it is easy to get off track in pursuing a coherent vision. This is the time you *most* need to do this exercise.

Why are some executives reluctant to do this? During periods of adversity and change, some leaders may have a tendency to feel defensive—they want to project that they "have the answers" and don't want to appear to be tentative or uncertain. Maybe there is an element of "denial" that creeps in, or fear of confronting the fact that certain "mistakes" might have been made. Leaders need to be aware of these tendencies and push themselves to overcome them.

Very often, as a result of this exercise, leaders realize how critical a shared vision among their senior leadership group is to decision making, strategy formulation, and key trade-offs. A typical reaction that I hear from the executives assembled in those rooms is, "I wish we had done this exercise years ago! It could have saved us hundreds of hours of debate, disagreement, and confusion." They tell me that it could have helped save money, stop the erosion of their competitive position, and focus them on the key initiatives necessary for them to succeed.

A Biotech Impasse

The CEO of a midsize biotech company was very pleased that his company was making great progress on two key drugs it had been developing, but at the same time, was frustrated by—and quite worried about—ongoing disagreements among his senior leadership team. First and foremost, the team couldn't agree on what additional compounds they should be developing. Factions had developed within the company based on this disagreement, and the CEO didn't know how to break the impasse.

Meanwhile, he also felt strongly that, given the company's cash burn rate and forward research agenda, they needed to raise additional capital over the next year. While this could take the form of a joint venture, private placement, or IPO, he was quite convinced that the company needed to take some action to bolster its financial resources. On this issue, there was severe disagreement and tension within the company's senior leadership ranks. Many were suspicious about the CEO's motives in wanting to raise capital so soon after their last round of venture financing. Here, too, the CEO was becoming alarmed about his inability to mobilize his senior leadership, resolve these issues, and move the group forward.

After listening to him explain the situation, I asked him to articulate the vision for the company. He looked at me with obvious skepticism and then dutifully recited a few boilerplate platitudes having to do with values, ethics, and key practices.

I told him that, despite his clear recitation, I didn't hear a *vision* in his laundry list of platitudes.

Somewhat annoyed, he tried again to explain. This time, as he avoided the boilerplate lingo, he struggled even more. That struggle, and our subsequent discussion, helped him realize that he had not developed a clearly articulated aspiration for the company. Yes, they wanted to develop a commercially viable drug. Yes, they wanted to build a strong company and make money. But, *why* did they want to develop a drug and build a strong company?

Frustrated and exasperated, he asked me why this mattered. He wanted to discuss the problems he was having at the company. Why did I insist on diverting him to this discussion? I reiterated some of the arguments outlined above. Gradually, he began to realize that the lack of a clear and compelling vision might well be *at the core of his problems*. If he couldn't explain the vision, maybe his senior leaders couldn't explain it either. If that was true, how could they be expected to agree on key decisions critical to the future direction of the company? He realized he needed to reexamine his efforts to develop a clear aspiration for his company.

We decided to try an experiment. I met in a hotel conference room with him and his top fifteen leaders. I had several large whiteboards at the front of the room. I asked several of the key questions listed above: What do you want to be able to tell your children fifteen years from now about why you worked here? What would you like the company to look like ten years from now? I asked several additional questions that were specific to this company's circumstances, and paid close attention as each member of the group gave his or her views and listened to each other.

It was an enlightening exercise for everyone in the room. Even though this group had been together for ten years, they realized they didn't know each other as well as they had thought—and that they had stopped really listening to each other several years ago.

From their comments, I wrote a vision statement on the board. The essence of their vision was to *build a company of superb researchers dedicated to finding treatments for disease*. That's why they were working so hard to develop compounds and build the company. This vision was based on their dreams, as well as on their realistic assessment of their key distinctive competencies. I asked them to critique and reshape what I had written until there was a basic agreement within the group.

This exercise took approximately two hours. Then, on the basis of that discussion, we discussed and debated the key priorities that were critical to achieving this vision. Over the next sixty minutes, they debated and eventually agreed on which compounds to pursue and which *not* to pursue. It was clear to them that certain compounds were more likely to be translated into treatments than others, and they concluded only those that could be translated should be pursued. They also agreed on how and when to raise capital. They realized the tight connection between achieving their shared vision and raising sufficient capital to achieve it. They dramatically improved their understanding of why the CEO had been pushing for additional financing. Their shared vision of developing actual treatments would require financial staying power—hence, the issue wasn't *whether* to do it, but *how* to do it.

It was surprisingly easy to resolve these core issues, once they had agreed on a vision. The CEO was amazed. He now understood that they hadn't really been fighting over the specific issues at hand. Instead, they had been using those issues as proxies for more basic issues. Really, they were fighting because each had a different conception of what the aspiration of the company ought to be. Once they reached consensus on that issue, the micro issues were relatively easy to resolve. Since that time, the company has pursued a very successful strategy. In addition, I hear from the senior executives that the leadership group now functions far more effectively as a team, which has allowed it to improve its ability to confront issues and make course adjustments as needed.

I have seen this same scene play out time and time again, with leaders of businesses, nonprofit organizations, and government agencies. In each case, I have been struck by the power of a clear vision that is shared by leadership and whole organizations. It clarifies disputes, informs various levels of the organization about what is truly important, and is a powerful motivator. As the prior example illustrates, it sets the stage for the next step: the identification of key priorities.

Defining the Key Priorities

Vision is critical, but alone, it is not sufficient. You also need a specific road map.

A vision must also be accompanied by a manageable number of top priorities that, if adhered to, will enable you and your organization to achieve your aspirations. Key priorities tell you and your colleagues what tasks they must perform superbly in order to make your vision come to life. A short list of essential priorities identifies those key tasks that deserve a disproportionate share of your time and focus.

You Have to Consciously Make Choices

Priorities inherently involve choices. You have only twenty-four hours in a day, and you have only a finite amount of human and financial capital. As a result, the development of key priorities takes a meaningful amount of thought and reflection. It is easy to develop a list of fifteen to twenty priorities, but I would argue that this is the same as having *no* priorities. Human beings typically can perform at a high level only if they focus their efforts, and the greater the number of priorities you have, the harder it becomes to focus. A long list means that you're avoiding the tough choices.

It is often quite difficult to identify the most critical three to five priorities and make the commitment to allocate your time and resources to achieving them. These priorities become the tasks that you intensively drive against. At the same time, you're implicitly defining what is less important, and even unimportant.

I find it useful to categorize key tasks into 1s, 2s, and 3s. The 1s are tasks you must do superbly to succeed. The 2s need to be done, but not necessarily at an optimal level. The 3s might be nice to do, but you'll live if they slip or are not even done at all. I often use the term *optimal* versus *sufficient*. Which tasks do you need to do at an optimal level (i.e., your very best) and which simply need to be done at a sufficient level (i.e., they should be done, but the level of quality is not so critical)?

In order to narrow the list down to three to five priorities, you might try to categorize them into these three buckets and ultimately zero in on the question "What are the *critical tasks we must do superbly if we are to achieve our vision?*"

Leading a Sales Force: Priorities Matter

The national sales force manager of a very large consumer goods company was frustrated that his regional leaders were not achieving their respective regional sales goals. He felt under a good deal of pressure to improve sales performance and had been communicating that anxiety to his managers. I asked him to enumerate the three to five top priorities that were critical for his sales managers to pursue in order to improve sales. He responded, "Well, it's not realistic to boil the job down to three to five priorities. There are at least fifteen priorities, and it wouldn't be appropriate to narrow the list down to, say, five."

Wow, you can't even narrow it down to five? Out loud, I observed that if I worked for him, I honestly would not know where to focus my time. He made it clear that he didn't agree. On the other hand, he let me interview some of his sales managers, and—as I had anticipated—they didn't know what he wanted them to do. He hadn't pushed himself to prioritize which tasks were most critical in order to drive sales, and—without an impetus from him—they hadn't picked a consistent set of priorities, either. I also observed that there were certain tasks that seemed minor but took a substantial amount of their time. No, they told me; they couldn't explain how these tasks connected to increased sales, but they were part of the company's customary practices.

The national sales manager decided to take some time to think about this issue. It required several weeks of thought, consultation with his best sales managers, and reflection on his own sales career. He finally identified four priorities that were critical, if they were going to meet their sales growth targets.

The most important of these was a large customer-targeting exercise, through which they would identify those accounts where they were underpenetrated, and then develop a specific coverage strategy/action plan to "attack" each account. This plan was clear and actionable. The sales force did an excellent job of executing it, and it ultimately led to a clear improvement in sales performance. It turned out that, in this business, 80 percent of the sales (and profits) came from large customers. They were harder to crack than smaller accounts, and so the sales force tended to give equal focus to large and small accounts. In order to overcome this tendency, the sales manager needed to make large accounts a clear priority. In addition, he deemphasized a number of time-consuming practices that were not critical to achieving the company's current sales goals.

Making Trade-off Decisions Based on Your Vision

To reiterate, *having fifteen priorities is the same as having none.* How many do you and your team have? How many of these priorities are holdovers from a previous era? As a manager, you have the responsibility to translate the vision into a manageable number of actionable priorities.

Examples of key priorities might include:

- Innovation/new product development. We want to be superb at developing new products and services. We are willing to allocate funds, as well as a material amount of human capital, to enhance our ability to innovate. The CEO and senior leadership are willing to make sacrifices, contribute people resources as appropriate, and communicate that this is a critical function within the company. Metrics will be developed that measure "success" in this area. This priority will affect decisions regarding key hires, how innovation will be organized (i.e., separated from, or integrated with, other functions), and how innovation will be rewarded. In addition, leadership will have to determine what kind of culture will best foster development of innovation. Also, leadership will need to determine the role of all company employees in this priority.

- Customer relationships and service. To achieve our goals, how strong must we be at product development as well as building client relationships? How critical are relationships to this sell? How critical is understanding and providing solutions to customer needs? Are we a product company or a client solutions company—or both? What is our distinctive competence—combining various products to solve problems or creating a single product line that fills a specific need as part of a broader set of solutions? Priorities here might include initiatives for recruiting a certain caliber of salesperson, organizing the sales force, and realigning compensation. As we'll discuss in the next chapter, these priorities will also dictate how much time the CEO spends with clients.

- Pricing. Are we the low-priced or premium-priced entry? This has substantial implications for our channels of distribution, product quality, degree of innovation, and so forth. If we intend to be low priced, priorities need to be developed to drive down product cost. If we intend to be premium priced, initiatives might include taking steps to develop our own channel of distribution in order to better control the customer experience—just as Apple did in 2001 by creating its own chain of retail stores.[6]

- Attracting, retaining, and developing the best people. How much time should the CEO spend on recruiting and coaching? This priority also involves initiatives to target and hire the level of quality and type of person necessary to staff the key business units of the firm, given the aspirations of those business units. This might also involve an initiative to train entry-level people, as well as key management professionals. (Starting several decades ago, General Electric has made this a critical priority, establishing and nurturing its Crotonville training center to help accomplish this goal.[7]) Finally, an initiative to coach and mentor key staff might be a top priority for a company highly dependent on key talent.

One Size Does Not Fit All

Every function, business unit, and geographic region has its own unique characteristics. While a company should have a core vision and shared key priorities, each unit should adapt the vision and priorities to fit its particular role in the company's success.

For example, the sales department is likely to have priorities that focus on customer penetration, sales performance, service, and its staff. The IT department might focus on how to develop the key technology support that will allow each of the company's divisions to achieve its key objectives. Manufacturing might have key priorities involving process improvements, product quality, and similar issues.

Typically, a company establishes its overarching priorities, and then those priorities are translated into key priorities by each unit. In most companies, these priorities are set through an annual business planning process that cascades through the organization.

Globalization: Priorities Must Be Adapted Regionally

The CEO of a global professional services firm was particularly concerned about his company's lack of progress in building its business in the Asia Pacific region. In prior years, it had been quite successful in the United States, so it had decided that its strategy would be to bring to Asia those qualities that had made the firm so successful in the United States.

The company first tried hiring locals to lead the business, but found that it couldn't build a strong leadership team with that approach. It then sent several leaders from the United States to Asia and put them in charge of the business. It had been a difficult process, in part because the expatriates who had been sent over to Asia often did not want to stay for longer than five years, at the end of which new expatriates had to be transferred to take their place. The net result of this and other problems was that the firm's market penetration had been poor, relative to its other U.S. and global competitors.

When we sat down to discuss these challenges, I asked the CEO to detail the vision and key priorities for the Asia Pacific business. In response, he showed me the firm's global priorities and said that each region had been handed down its marching orders from headquarters. I asked how much he adapted these priorities to fit the local culture, business environment, competitive dynamics, customer needs, and the like. He said that in light of the company's success in the United States, its approach was to take what worked there and export those practices to Asia. He argued strongly that this was the right approach.

We took a trip to the region together and then talked again over the course of several days. Partly as a result of our trip, he came to appreciate that each country in the Asia Pacific region was different from the others, and certainly different from the United States. Clearly, from country to country, cultures differed, customer needs differed, hiring practices differed, and so on. Unfortunately, the company was ignoring these differences and as a result was failing to effectively adapt to them.

We worked on this for several months. Gradually, the company's leaders concluded that they needed to tailor their plans much more tightly to the region. They also realized that they needed to immediately establish a priority of recruiting indigenous talent and grooming these local professionals to become senior leaders in the region. A key ingredient in this grooming would be a one- to two-year assignment in one of the U.S. businesses, followed by a transfer back to a key leadership post in the region. This would allow the indigenous hire to learn deeply about the company and its culture. It would, in turn, help the company better understand each local country, better penetrate clients, and tailor its business strategies to fit the local needs, rather than pushing its U.S. strategy on Asia.

These priorities would take years to achieve. But the company's leaders had a newfound confidence that they were now on a path that would give them a much higher chance of success—and which would allow them to better achieve their overall company vision of global leadership.

Communication, and *Overcommunication,* Is Critical

Once you have developed a vision with specific important priorities, you must communicate, and then overcommunicate, these messages.

Employees and other constituents are acutely aware of the contextual changes that are happening every day in and around the business. These may be changes in the economy, actions of competitors, fundamental behavioral changes among customers or clients, changes in the leadership of the organization, or one of a myriad of other variables.

As a result, they want to know, "Is our vision still the same? Are our key priorities still the same? Should I be changing what I'm doing? How can I help? How will I be evaluated? If I have to make a spot decision under time pressure, and I can't check with a senior person, what should I do? Do I know enough to make critical decisions if I need to?"

My strong advice for leaders is, as often as you think you communicate a vision with priorities, *it is almost certainly not enough to meet the needs of your people*.

The senior leaders of a large, well-managed professional services firm prided themselves on having a clear vision and a short list of specifically articulated priorities for each of their business units. Employee surveys reflected high employee satisfaction, and the company rated highly on most questions. There was one clear exception: "Do you think you understand the strategy and priorities for your unit, and for the overall company?" On this question, the scores were surprisingly low.

I have seen this phenomenon repeatedly at companies I have worked with. Typically, the leaders express confusion and frustration in response to these low ratings. They believe in their hearts that they have been communicating the vision and priorities regularly, thoroughly, and effectively.

What's the truth? In most cases, it turns out that leaders don't communicate frequently enough, or deeply enough, for their employees to "get it." In the press of day-to-day activities, they don't adequately communicate the vision in a manner that helps their people understand what they're supposed to do to drive the business. Quarterly or biannual town hall meetings, a blurb in the annual report, or a static page on the company Web site are simply not sufficient.

In Times of Severe Change, Multiply Your Frequency of Communication

This deficiency has become all the more troublesome in recent years, when economic conditions have been changing by the week, the day, or even the hour. Human nature causes leaders to communicate less in periods of uncertainty: "I'm not sure what to say!" But the truth is, it's exactly then—during these stressful periods—that the leader really needs to overcommunicate the vision and key priorities. If there are troubling uncertainties, fine; acknowledge them. But always come back to what you want your people to be doing during this difficult period.

Could your employees recite the vision and priorities for your company or business unit? Try this test with your people. If they seem unsure, I would encourage you to *multiply by five* the number of times you communicate the vision and priorities. In other words, take advantage of every opportunity that you have to meet with your people to rearticulate the vision and priorities. Ideally, you should also be clear (and communicate through your body language) that you are ready to answer any questions that they may have, and that you're available to help clear up any confusion, uncertainties, or misunderstandings.

How much is enough? When I was in the hot seat, I used to say to myself (only half-jokingly) that the acid test was, "Repeat it enough that employees start to anticipate and mimic you." In other words, articulate this message so often that employees begin to say, "Here comes Mr./Ms. X; get ready for the vision and key priorities A, B, and C!"

In addition to communicating these messages yourself, you should make sure that your senior leaders are also doing the same with their direct reports and employees. In my career, I sometimes found it useful to boil down my "stump speech" into a number of bullet points that could be printed on a laminated card that fit in a wallet (or could be pinned on the wall). In this way, I could help ensure that the organization was mobilizing around a specific vision and related priorities.

Dynamism and Change

One final observation: vision and priorities are not static. Priorities change frequently in response to specific challenges and opportunities. Visions shouldn't change with every shifting wind—they should provide continuity in difficult times—but eventually, they too are likely to be rethought. The world changes and you must adapt to that change.

The Cystic Fibrosis Foundation (CFF) was founded more than fifty years ago to help find treatments for cystic fibrosis, a relatively rare hereditary disease that initially afflicts infants. At the time of CFF's founding, its vision to find treatments led the foundation to focus on (1) raising money and (2) establishing research centers at various academic institutions in the United States that were already conducting CF research.

As CFF made progress in research and treatments, patient life expectancies increased from only one year to more than thirty years. As a result, the vision for the organization evolved. Henceforth, the foundation would not only focus on treatments, but also attempt to improve the quality of life for patients living with the disease. Raising money and funding promising research remained a priority, but a new critical priority now emerged: creating a pharmacy service that ensured that patients were counseled and treated with the proper medicines. As the organization became more complex, it also established a priority to create a more professional executive team and organization—meaning the recruitment of extremely high-quality staff and the centralization of key business functions.

At every stage of its development, the foundation's board of directors and CEO have been willing to debate and re-debate their vision. On the basis of that vision, they've made the tough trade-off decisions, identifying three to five key priorities at which they needed to excel in order to achieve their goals. This process of establishing and reestablishing the vision, and establishing and reestablishing key priorities, is a key reason why this nonprofit has been so successful in raising money, developing treatments, and improving the quality of life (and longevity) of cystic fibrosis patients.[8]

The larger point is *change*: what worked well in the past may not work so well in the future. The world is changing at a faster pace than ever before. Globalization, technological innovation, and economic cycles require leaders (and their organizations) to adapt. In addition, unforeseen crises occur, and when they do, the priorities of the leader must change.

Crises Can Reshape and Reorder Priorities

The terrible BP oil spill of 2010 required a change in priorities for several leaders involved. The CEO and senior leadership of BP had to reorient much of their energy and focus on stopping the leak, cleaning up the spill, compensating victims, and communicating the company's priorities and plans. Almost overnight, no single priority was more critical to the future of the company than dealing with this spill. The company's leadership had to reprioritize—and how well it succeeded (or didn't succeed) will have a profound impact on the reputation and future of this company.

Concurrently, the governors in the region had to completely reallocate key resources to meet the priorities of (1) cleanup and (2) advocacy for their states in Washington. At the same time, they had to communicate to their constituents that they were "on top of" the situation.

For his part, President Obama had just finished a bruising health-care reform battle and was preoccupied with a host of concerns, including passing financial reform, fighting wars in Afghanistan and Iraq, and trying to deal with a fragile economy. Out of the blue, his administration and the Department of the Interior had to make this spill a top priority, and it became critical that they forcefully communicate to the country that this spill had become a top priority. Some critics argued that the Obama team was slow to reprioritize—and slow to communicate the reprioritization—and therefore lost valuable time and credibility.

During the recent economic crisis, countless business managers and nonprofit leaders had to reposition their organizations to adapt to changing conditions. At Harvard, I taught a substantial number of owner-managers of small and medium-size companies during this period. In 2008 and early 2009, a steady stream came to my office asking variations of the same question.

"We need to cut back expenses due to a 30 percent reduction in our revenues," they would say. "I've identified several different options, but I'm not sure which way to go."

In each case, we started with discussing and defining their distinctive competencies and their vision for the business. We debated whether those competencies still prevailed. In some cases, the business leader realized that his or her company realistically had one or two key competencies, yet during the previous boom economic times, they migrated to actively pursuing businesses that were based on three or four. They understood that they had to face reality regarding what they were truly great at, cut back in those areas where they were unlikely to have a sustainable competitive advantage, alter their vision if necessary, and reorder the priorities they were driving to pursue.

Across various industries and geographic regions, this type of reorientation exercise occurred frequently. Those companies that were able to face reality, restructure, and refocus around core competencies dramatically increased their chances of surviving and emerging even stronger. Those that didn't lost a critical opportunity and further turned the odds against themselves.

Downturns force you to do this exercise. You shouldn't wait for a crisis, though, to perform this analysis and take the necessary steps to update your vision and priorities. I often use the analogy of the middle-aged man who is walking around knowing that he is 50 pounds overweight. Should he wait for a heart attack to address his condition? Of course not! While a crisis provides valuable motivation, it can be too late to take action to save the patient. Similarly, an organization should not wait for a severe crisis before it takes action.

Crises normally take root during periods that seem safe, stable, and profitable. In other words, while crises appear to come out of nowhere, they typically take years to develop, and most often stem from a failure to face reality and update visions and key priorities. You want to proactively and deliberately revisit these issues when times are good, so that you can calmly and carefully think through these issues without having to act under severe pressure.

A Key Building Block—First Things First

The development of a vision and associated priorities is a fundamental building block in subsequent chapters of this book—and far more important, for the success of your business. With this foundation in place, it will be much more obvious how you should execute the concepts and ideas you are about to read in the next chapters. In other words, you need to first know where you're going before you can answer most of the other key questions posed in this book.

Executives sometimes underestimate the importance of carefully building this foundation. Alternatively, they make the mistake of thinking that a quick "once-over" is sufficient. "I've got this covered," they tend to say early in our discussions. "Let's move on and talk about the more pressing issues I'm facing." My response in many such cases is, "I don't think you're going to be able to address those other pressing issues if you don't deal with this one first. I don't think I know where you want to take this organization, and I'm getting the strong impression that your people don't, either. There *is* no more pressing issue than this, and a quick pass through isn't going to cut it."

Why? Because a clearly articulated vision, translated into specific and compelling priorities, is a key ingredient in rallying a group to accomplish great things. Conversely, the lack of such a foundation can limit the potential of an extraordinary group of people and undermine the accomplishments of an otherwise superb company.

Suggested Follow-up Steps

1. Write down, in three to four sentences, a clear vision for your enterprise or business unit. (If it's helpful, use the exercises described earlier in this chapter.)

2. List the three to five key priorities that are most critical to achieving this vision. These should be tasks that you must do extraordinarily well in order for you to succeed based on where you are positioned today. (If you are having trouble narrowing them down to three to five, use the "1s, 2s, 3s" exercise described in this chapter.)

3. Ask yourself whether the vision (with priorities) is sufficiently clear and understandable. In addition, ask yourself whether you communicate the vision and priorities frequently enough that your key stakeholders (e.g., direct reports and employees) could repeat them back to you. Interview key employees to see whether they understand and can clearly rearticulate the vision and priorities.

4. Identify venues and occasions for the regular communication, reiteration, and discussion of the vision and priorities. Create opportunities for questions and answers.

5. Assemble your executive team off-site to debate the vision and priorities. In particular, consider whether the vision and priorities still fit the competitive environment, changes in the world, and the needs of the business. Use the off-site to update your vision and priorities and to ensure buy-in on the part of your senior leadership team.

2

Managing Your Time

How You Spend Your Time Should Flow Directly from Your Vision and Key Priorities

> **Do you know how you spend your time?**
> **Does it match your key priorities?**

When leaders are struggling, there is very often a mismatch between how they are spending their time and the most pressing needs of their business. A common consequence of this mismatch is that critical initiatives are not being sufficiently emphasized, and as a result, the firm is drifting off course. The symptoms of this situation are often quite evident, even if the leader is not yet aware that the way he is spending his time is a key contributor to the problem. For you to be an effective leader, your vision and key priorities must directly shape how you allocate your time.

There are a number of reasons why leaders fail to recognize when they are misallocating their time. First, amid the chaos of daily events and crises, it's easy for them to lose track of how they're actually spending their time. Second, many leaders have not explicitly identified their top three to five priorities, as recommended in the previous chapter, and therefore don't work to match up their efforts with these priorities. These executives may sense that they're not using their time effectively, but they're often not sure how to think about spending it more wisely. In addition, for a number of reasons, many executives simply have trouble saying no to requests for their time. As a result, they allow people and events to pull or push them into poor choices regarding how they expend their energies.

The purpose of this chapter is, first, to emphasize and remind you that your time is typically your most scarce and valuable asset—and you need to allocate it with a keen awareness of this fact. This starts with devising ways to measure how you're *actually spending your time*. Once you've done this, the next step is to compare how you are allocating your efforts with an updated distillation of your key priorities. We'll explore various approaches that may help you be more effective at this, and help you do a better job of organizing your schedule to drive key initiatives.

The second part of this chapter will discuss the leader's time allocation as an important signal to employees and other constituencies regarding what activities are truly valued in the overall organization as well as in individual business units. In addition, we will examine the importance of developing ongoing processes to make sure that your subordinates are effectively managing their time in order to achieve key priorities. Finally, I will ask you to consider the importance of facing and overcoming impediments to this overall effort.

Nothing Is More Valuable Than Your Time

Your time—and that of your people—is the most important asset you have. It is a finite asset and, once spent, cannot be replenished. Of course, many other assets are critical to the success of your organization: financial resources, franchise assets, real estate, and others. Your ability to deploy those assets effectively and create value, however, depends in large part on how wisely you spend your time and that of your people.

Despite their strong agreement with this concept, many business leaders—ranging from young professionals to senior executives—don't actually know how they spend their time. Try to recollect how you spent your time this last week. If I asked you to break down the time by categories of tasks, would you be able to produce a relatively accurate accounting?

Now imagine that I asked you to detail how you spent several thousand dollars of your own money this past month. Could you answer with some precision? I bet that, no matter what your income bracket, your answer would be a resounding yes! Most likely, you would have considered this expenditure carefully before you made it. You certainly would not have allowed yourself to get pulled or pushed into it just because you were having a busy week. You would likely have kept records of that spending and probably even tracked how satisfied you were with the impact or results.

It would have been important to you, and your actions would have underscored that fact. The fact is, *your time is every bit as important as your money*—probably more so. As a result, you need to adjust your mind-set to ensure that you behave accordingly.

Plan It, Track It, and Assess It

If you suspect that you are squandering your valuable time, a good next step would be to create analytical processes to systematically track it. I believe this approach can be extraordinarily useful to young professionals and emerging leaders, as well as to very senior executives. Here's a simple but effective exercise I have used myself and recommended to numerous professionals. For two weeks, use a spreadsheet to document how you spend every hour of your on-the-job time. Break it into categories that are relevant to your daily work life. You might want to use a "trial run" day to come up with the right action categories, such as:

Strategic planning

Client contact (including written, face-to-face, and phone)

Other sales and marketing

Interactions with investors and board members

Interactions with media

Supervision of direct reports (including coaching, mentoring, and reviews)

Management by walking around (the office or the manufacturing floor)

Competitive analysis

Recruitment

Innovation (product, process, or other)

Communications/interactions with employees (meetings, speeches, etc.)

Budgeting

Reviewing expenses, including looking at travel and expense reports

Scheduling yourself

Other administrative matters

Don't double-count hours; assign them to one category or another. (You're aiming for a coherent picture of how you're spending your time; it's fine to err on the side of simplicity.) At the end of the two weeks—ten working days—add up the hours in each of your categories. If it helps, break them down into percentages of your total time.

When I go through this exercise myself—and certainly, when I ask other executives to do it—the reaction is typically the same: surprise, and even shock, at the results. Why? Most often, people realize to their dismay that they are spending a great deal of their time on matters that, by any reasonable measure, are *not* critical to the performance of their job and the success of their enterprise.

Diagnosing the Mismatch— The Cost of Saying Yes

Once you've created an effective assessment of your current time allocation, it makes sense to consider why some of your time may be poorly spent. This is likely to require some introspection and deconstruction of the events and chaos of the workweek. We all know that life as a leader is *chaotic*. Events happen on their own schedule, and you are forced to respond.

Someone comes unannounced into your office with a problem and wants you to get involved; you may be reluctant to turn that person away. You see a situation developing that worries you and—even though you've delegated the responsibility—you decide to get directly involved and begin to nose around and ask questions. Even as you're undertaking this unscheduled assignment, the phone rings, and a colleague in another division is seeking your views on a given situation. He doesn't know who else to call, and he's hoping you'll get involved.

In these moments, there are lots of seemingly compelling reasons to get involved, starting with the fact that it feels *good* to be wanted. It feels good to have your opinion sought. You believe in yourself, and you're pretty sure that these situations will go better if you deal with them directly. You're afraid that if you say no, then folks won't come and seek you out as frequently and will think you're not very helpful. Maybe you'll be perceived as less important, or less capable, or less relevant.

Unfortunately, there is a cost to saying yes to calls on your time. If the task at hand is something that any number of other folks could have done, and if that task takes you away from things that you need to be spending time on and that only you can do, the cost is probably very high. It comes at the expense of things the organization really needs you to do.

For example: The CEO of a midsize manufacturing company was frustrated because he was working seventy hours a week and was feeling overwhelmed. He felt as if he were suffocating. He just couldn't catch up. His family life was deteriorating, and at work he was constantly unavailable for key critical initiatives involving his people and his major customers.

As a result, it seemed that everyone was annoyed and frustrated with him: his wife, his family, and his colleagues. "Where did I go wrong?" he asked me, genuinely baffled. "I worked my entire career to build the company to this level of size and market presence. I thought success would feel a lot more fun than this!"

Does any of this sound familiar to you? If so, you're not alone. In fact, it's a surprisingly typical scenario.

After discussing his vision and priorities for the business, I asked him to break down how he spent his time in a typical week. He thought about it for a minute or two and then admitted that he wasn't sure. We agreed that we'd speak again after he had taken the time needed to think about it. He then did the exercise of writing down the hour-by-hour breakdown of how he spent his time during the week.

When we next spoke, he took me through his analysis. As he reviewed the categories of his time, we both noticed that he was spending a substantial number of hours—approximately twelve hours a week—on something called "expense management." I asked him what that was, assuming that it might be hours devoted to cost reductions or process improvements. He explained that he approved all company expenditures in excess of $1,000. I asked him to discuss why he did this, given the fact that the business had approximately $500 million in sales revenue. "Well, in our first couple years in business," he replied, "sales were less than $5 million a year, and we were losing money. We watched every dollar like a hawk, and I made sure to approve these expenses. As we got larger, we felt it was important to maintain this strong expense management discipline."

I asked him whether there wasn't some other solution. For example, couldn't he delegate most of this responsibility to one of his direct reports, perhaps retaining responsibility for approval of expenditures over $50,000, or perhaps even $100,000?

He struggled to explain why he had not delegated at least some portion of this responsibility. As we talked about it, he realized that there was no compelling reason; it was just the way they had always done things. He acknowledged that by delegating the authority to approve recurring operating expenses below $50,000, he could reallocate as much as ten hours a week: an *enormous* savings of his time. With a chuckle, he commented, "I don't think it's unreasonable for me to learn to delegate these expense approvals so that I can focus on being a more effective CEO, husband, and father."

He reoriented his schedule and made the commitment to track his time going forward, so that he could achieve a better alignment between his time and his top priorities. He checked back with me several months later and reported significant progress—and not just in the expense-approval realm. He found himself more frequently running toward significant challenges and at the same time saying no to requests for his attention that could be handled by someone else. He felt that he was becoming more productive and therefore more vital to the business. Just as important, he was once again getting home at a reasonable hour.

Matching Time with Priorities

Once you have improved your ability to track and assess your time, the next step is to more explicitly match it to the key priorities of the organization. When executives are using their time poorly, it is very often because they haven't thought sufficiently about identifying the most important priorities for their particular company or business unit. In order to allocate their efforts more wisely, they have to first step back and pick their most important initiatives, and then circle back to match their time to these priorities.

In other cases, executives may have done an excellent job thinking through their priorities, but are not spending their time in a way that is aligned with successfully achieving their well-thought-out plans.

Thinking in 1s, 2s, and 3s

The CEO of a midsize manufacturing firm was feeling deeply frustrated. He felt overwhelmed by the task of building his business, which seemed to be slipping versus its key competitors. In coping with this situation, he was increasingly experiencing feelings of severe anxiety. Looking for answers, he came to Harvard to attend a one-week executive program. One afternoon early in the course, he came to my office in hopes of getting some insight into what was wrong.

When we sat down, he explained his company's competitive positioning and thought aloud about several possible explanations for the erosion of its business. Was his staff not up to the job? Maybe he had picked the wrong people. Was there a problem with the company's strategic plan? As he went through various hypotheses, he articulated his real fear: he wasn't a capable leader. He worried that he really wasn't up to the job.

"Do you think leaders are born, or made?" he finally asked me. "And if they're made, do you think *I* can learn to be a leader?"

After we had the vision and priorities discussion—which to his credit he had thought through very carefully over the years—I asked him to describe how he spent his time. As he spoke, I didn't really need to say very much at all. Pretty early in his accounting, he explained that he personally did some two dozen personnel reviews each year. He had retained the job of sales manager in the company, in part because he enjoyed traveling to pitches for large and small targets. He had also retained responsibility for the assistants and all administrative staff, which now included more than three hundred people.

While he felt quite comfortable doing these tasks, he also felt hard pressed to spend enough time on strategy and competitive analysis. This was critical, he believed, because two key competitors had recently merged, and this industry change most likely would create significant strategic challenges for his company's value proposition to their customers. His direct reports had been pressing him to focus on this, but he just couldn't find the time.

I asked him to do an exercise. I suggested he list the ways he spent time, and then allocate hours per week to each of those buckets. I also challenged him to put each hours-per-week number in one of three columns: column 1 being important tasks that only he could do and were essential to achieving the company's most critical priorities; column 2 being important tasks (based on critical priorities) but ones that could be accomplished, at least in part, by someone else; and column 3 representing tasks that were not critically important and should be done by someone else in the organization.

He came up with the chart in real time, and we then discussed each of the tasks he was spending time on. For example, he wrote down "dealing with administrative staff" and noted this was a 3, which took seven hours per week. "Going on small-account sales calls" consumed ten hours a week and also belonged in the 3 column. (He really wasn't needed on those calls.) "Doing two dozen performance reviews" consumed forty-five hours in the fall; half were 1s or 2s, and the other half were 3s. We continued through various other tasks until we accounted for 100 percent of his time.

As a result of seeing this analysis in black and white, he immediately resolved to actively delegate the 3s and closely examine which of the 2s had to be done by him. He also recognized that he should increase his allocation to some of the 1s. With the help of this very simple matrix, he concluded that he hadn't been sufficiently strategic or disciplined about using his time. He had wasted a lot of his time and energy on less important tasks and was failing to face up to the big competitive challenges that only he could spearhead! He also realized that, whatever his native skills, many leadership habits are "learned," and he had to learn to focus on the bigger issues and delegate the rest.

Six months later, he called me to report that he had very effectively reallocated his time. He had immersed himself more fully in assessing the company's competitive positioning and had concluded that it should merge with a key competitor. This was a difficult decision, but one he believed was essential to the company's future well-being—and one that couldn't have been made without his intense focus.

Getting out of Our Grooves

Over time, all of us can get sloppy. We drift into poor time management habits. This is why we have to step back and scrutinize our time allocations on some regular basis.

I am as guilty of this as the next person. When I first did this time allocation exercise myself, back in my early thirties, I discovered that I was spending five hours a week on scheduling. This was before today's scheduling software existed, so I'd spend a lot of time on the phone trying to find a day in the week, and an hour in that day, where a particular group of colleagues could get together for a meeting: "How about Wednesday? How about 2 p.m.? No? How about Thursday at 3? OK; hold that slot; I'll check with Joan, Tom, and Sam and get back to you."

It was frustrating, distracting, and a poor use of five hours a week. Worse, my assistant could do all this without me, and she could do it much better than I would. Finally, and belatedly, I went to her and said, "Sandy, from now on, you keep my calendar. Anyone who wants to schedule me, I will send to you, whenever possible." What a relief, and what a time savings! Overnight, I had more time, and my head was clearer to focus on other priorities.

As managers, leaders—and indeed, as humans—we get stuck in our grooves. We join a small company in which every task seems critically important—and of course, every task is done better if we do it ourselves. The company prospers and grows, we move up through the ranks, our time becomes ever more scarce and valuable—and yet, we don't focus enough on which tasks are critical for us to do and which tasks should be delegated to others (see further discussion in chapter 4).

We cling to our established habits and procedures long after they stop making sense—either for us or for the company. Those habits might once have been useful but are now counterproductive. We have to recognize that and strive to create new habits.

Time Management and Its Impact on the Leader as Role Model

I frequently ask leaders with whom I work to do this time-tracking exercise. Then I ask them to compare how their time is being spent in relation to the priorities they have identified for the business. (See the previous chapter.) Again, most leaders who feel that they are struggling—young and old alike—find that there is a significant mismatch.

What is the cost of this mismatch? First and most obvious, the leader is not as effective as he or she should be in driving critical priorities. Time spent going southwest is time *not* spent driving north (or whatever your intended direction is). Worse, as explained in a subsequent chapter, leaders are supposed to serve as a role model for the organization. If they don't spend time on the overriding priorities, it sends a strong signal that they really don't believe in those priorities. In an organizational setting, this can be poison.

How you spend your time speaks volumes about what you believe in, and what you want the organization to do. For example, if you have identified *developing top client relationships* as a critical priority, you need to demonstrate through your actions that you're serious about it. If you are consistently unavailable for critical client relationship calls, you strongly communicate to the organization that this really isn't such a high priority—or maybe that you believe it's important for *employees* to do, but not sufficiently important for someone on *your* level to worry about. You communicate the notion that, on the margin, employees can get away with skipping a significant client trip, or it's not that big a deal to miss a piece of business, or that it's OK for people at this company to be reactive with clients.

This can have a huge impact on the culture and on the intensity regarding this priority. It can make the difference between success and failure.

Think back to the last time that a boss asked you to do something that he or she obviously was unwilling to do him- or herself. How seriously did you take it? How seriously did the organization take it?

I grew up in a professional services firm. We identified attracting, retaining, and developing superb talent as a critical priority. As a junior person, I was enormously impressed that very senior leaders of the firm were willing to interview candidates and attend recruiting events on a regular basis. I learned from their example that there wasn't anything more important than recruiting and developing talent.

When I became a senior leader, I made sure to allocate a material amount of my time to this pursuit. It spoke louder than any speech I could have ever given, and helped build our firm into a powerhouse operation. I learned that, up and down the organization, people are closely observing your behavior and looking for clear and positive signals about what is truly valued. How you, as a leader, spend your time sends an enormously powerful signal.

Do as I Say, Not as I Do: Mixed Messages from the CEO

The CEO of a rapidly growing industrial products firm was struggling to accomplish one of his key priorities. By way of background, his father was the founder of the business, and this CEO was the second generation of his family to lead the company. The business had started with a specific machine tool that was critical to its customers' manufacturing processes. Over the years, the company had branched out into various product adjacencies, and in recent years, it had begun to provide more custom-tailored machine tool solutions to its customers as a way to further differentiate itself from its competitors.

As a result of this initiative, one significant and relatively new priority was *to better understand customer needs*. This involved developing a more in-depth understanding of customers' overall business strategy, and how each of their manufacturing processes was evolving to meet their own end-user customer needs. This, in turn, meant upgrading the sophistication of the company's sales force and providing substantially more technical support for the sales force. (They had to become *consultants* as well as salespeople.) But there was a problem: the people in the business were extremely skeptical about the leadership's commitment to pursuing this initiative.

The CEO gave a number of speeches about the importance of this effort and was frustrated by the skepticism that kept coming back at him. When he came to see me to discuss this situation, I asked him how he was spending his *own* time. As is often the case, he wasn't immediately able to answer. Subsequently, he tracked his time for a week. He reported that he was surprised to find how much of his time was spent on administrative activities and also on one money-losing product line that was a core part of the company's original legacy.

What was the problem, here? The CEO was paying a great deal of attention to things that didn't reflect the business's priorities. Worse than that, his excessive focus on the legacy business—even though it was now a money loser and was unlikely to regain profitability—suggested that he was more driven by emotion and sentimentality than by business logic. Upon reflection, he began to realize that he needed to be far more disciplined as a leader and as a role model.

He immediately began pushing himself to delegate a number of his second- and third-tier administrative tasks. He asked a trusted lieutenant to begin thinking about what to do about the legacy business—up to and including closing it down—and substantially increased the amount of time he spent on the road talking with important customers. These changes set a powerful and very encouraging example for his people.

After making these changes, the CEO reported notable improvements in the company's efforts to better understand its own customers. His time on the road inspired and helped young salespeople and helped persuade them to implement the new account-management initiative. As a result, he felt dramatically more comfortable with the strategic positioning of his business and his own effectiveness as CEO.

The Time Match Exercise

Matching time allocation with major priorities should be an ongoing management exercise for you. It helps you figure out what you should delegate and what you really need to do yourself. In many cases, it gives you the backbone to say no to requests for your time that don't fit—and, at the same time, figure out which situations you really do need to involve yourself in (whether invited or not!). It may also have the added benefit of empowering your employees to do a number of tasks themselves—rather than coming to you with problems they can really resolve themselves—freeing you up to spend your time on those tasks where you're most needed.

Again: the best test is to ask yourself, "Could other people in the organization do this same task?" If the answer is yes, then you should *not* be doing it. You should be looking to spend time on those activities that fit your key priorities and require your personal involvement—whether it's identifying and making critical decisions, building major client relationships, coaching senior staff, or rethinking the strategy.

What Do I Enjoy? Am I in the Right Job?

One final thought for this section: this time allocation exercise only makes sense if you're *honest* with yourself. You have to be honest, maybe even a bit cold blooded, in assessing the results.

Some people I've worked with have ultimately confessed that they have a certain activity that they've always done, and that they really enjoy, but that no longer fits with the needs of their current job or the needs of the organization. They "protect" that activity because they enjoy it.

This is, of course, understandable. If you can't square your organization's priorities with your professional interests, however, you may be in the wrong job. If you're in the wrong job, deal with *that* challenge. Rewrite the job description. Sometimes, this may involve looking inside or even outside the company for a new job.

By the same token, when you are looking for a new job or are offered a job within your company, you should ask what are the three to five key tasks that you'll need to focus on to be outstanding in that position. Do you enjoy those activities?

Looked at from the other side of the table, successful companies find a way to match employee skills and passions with critical leadership jobs in the organization. This fit helps individuals succeed and helps companies reach their potential.

A Management Exercise for Your People

I recently spent time with the CEO of a very well-run health-care services firm. After years of practice, he learned to do an outstanding job matching his time to the organization's top priorities.

He also took the next logical step, directing each of his senior managers to do a similar time allocation exercise to ensure they were matching their time to major priorities. Largely as a result of this discipline, the company is very adept at aligning and then realigning against key priorities, as those priorities evolve to achieve the vision of the firm.

This is an excellent practice. Ask your people to do the exercise of matching their time with your organization's top priorities. It drives home what tasks are critical and how they should spend their time. It helps make the distinction between what time allocation is critical, what is simply "nice to do," and what may actually be counterproductive. It may suggest where they can afford to cut or—conversely—where they may need to add to their resources and staff.

Beyond resource allocation, this exercise gives you a solid basis for coaching your people throughout the year and also for evaluating them at year-end. They won't have to wonder what you're looking for, in terms of priorities and time allocation, because you've been clear about that all along.

Time Allocation Needs to Be Dynamic

We often get into trouble (and encounter new opportunities) because things change. You almost certainly will encounter changes in the external environment. Most industries go through cycles; you may be subject to those cycles. Most product lines ultimately mature; your products may be commoditized, or perhaps your patents are expiring.

Over the previous decades, we have watched airlines, pharmaceutical companies, financial services firms, insurance companies, auto manufacturers, and countless other industries being forced to come to grips with fundamental changes in the regulatory environment, emergence of global competitors, changes in consumer preferences, and the like. In these cases, senior leadership teams were compelled to adapt their company's visions, reestablish new priorities, and reorient how they spent their time.

In addition to this, depending on your business, you may experience seasonal changes that require you to "make hay while the sun shines" and hunker down during the slower months. Many segments of the retail industry are classic examples of this type of seasonality. For example, the jewelry industry has its busy seasons in the months leading up to Valentine's Day and Christmas. During those months, the emphasis is on serving customers, hiring peak store help, merchandising, and getting delivery on specialty inventory items. In the off-peak months, the leadership often focuses more on collecting on customer receivables, initiating new product designs for the following year, and running sales to clear slow-moving merchandise.

In short, it is the story of business: companies and industries change, and either adapt or ultimately fail. Similarly, their leaders also must reassess and change the way they spend their time if they are to survive and prosper.

The key point here is that time allocation needs to be done on a continuing basis. It's important to ask yourself this question periodically. Just as you would step back and review a major investment decision at some regular interval, you need to dispassionately review the manner in which you invest your time.

Facing and Overcoming the Disconnect

Does this chapter resonate with you?

You may already have an excellent handle on time management. Perhaps you do a fine job of matching how you spend your time with key priorities, and with the stage and season of your business.

Alternatively, you may believe that you just don't have the time to focus on this effort. If so, I would suggest that you re-examine this view. I have listened politely to more than a few executives who have told me, in so many words, "Listen, I don't have the time to spend on these exercises because I am *just too busy!*" To them, this effort seemed separate from or marginal to the execution of their job responsibilities. They didn't see that much of the chaos they were experiencing was a *direct result* of their failure to analyze, prioritize, and allocate their time to key tasks.

At the same time, many of these individuals were complaining about having enormous difficulty living up to their past successes or finding a path toward new successes—individually or organizationally.

When faced with this kind of disconnect—between what someone so obviously needs to do and what he or she is willing to do—I often suggest that the struggling manager revisit the kinds of issues raised in this chapter. I also suggest they take a vacation or find some other way to get away and get perspective on their lives. Some people balk at this suggestion, claiming that they simply *lack the time*. I persist: "Isn't it true that you are constantly and unsuccessfully fighting the chaos of the workplace? Why are you so unhappy? Why do you think you're so frustrated with what you're able to accomplish at work—particularly when, as the boss, you have the ability to make just about any change you wish to make?"

Many years ago, I read a book by author Stephen Covey— *The Seven Habits of Highly Effective People*—which introduced a simple two-by-two matrix that captures the essence of this dilemma.[1] One axis of Covey's grid is "urgency" (going from high urgency to low urgency) and the other is "importance" (going from important to unimportant). The sweet spots in Covey's grid are urgent/important and important/not urgent; everything else is at best a distraction, and at worst, a waste of time.

Why do smart and skilled people insist on hanging out in the "wrong" quadrants of that grid—zones that are full of distractions and time wasters? After thinking about this issue for several years, I would make two general observations:

- We have trouble saying no for admirable reasons. We have a hard time turning away the kinds of inquiries, requests, and tiny opportunities that pop up in the course of almost every workday. Why? In part because we're taught from childhood to be helpful. (Think of the first six characteristics that a Boy Scout is asked to swear to: *trustworthy, loyal, helpful, friendly, courteous,* and *kind*—a prescription for getting overextended!) And frankly, most people—myself included—enjoy being asked to get involved in something. That's a signal that someone admires something about you and that they think their problem will benefit from your attention. Again, these are all things that make it harder to say no—even when we should.

- We have trouble saying no for less admirable reasons. Maybe we are control freaks: unable to take or keep our hands off of things. Maybe we aren't good at delegating because we don't trust our people, or we don't trust ourselves. I had many colleagues during my banking career who were convinced that they had to be personally involved for a particular job to be done properly.

One technique that I have found valuable for most of my career has been to write down on a piece of paper my three to five most critical priorities. These are usually a combination of major business priorities and also one or more personal development priorities (e.g., spend more time being a better listener or spend more time coaching subordinates). I keep this sheet pinned to my office wall so that I can see it every day. When someone arrives at my doorstep and asks me to take something on, I look at that sheet on the wall before I make a decision.

Try this, and before you respond to the request, ask yourself whether you should:

- Get involved, knowing that this will represent time away from your priorities and may result in your getting spread too thin.

- Decline to get involved, and suggest that your visitor try again to solve it on his or her own. He can always come back to you for help if he's unable to resolve it himself.

- Decline to get involved, but recommend that your visitor involve a third colleague who might be another resource for getting this problem resolved. (If this third colleague reports to you, this might be a good chance to work on your delegation skills, the subject of a subsequent chapter.)

There's no "right" answer, but—as the list above suggests— you are probably wise to lean toward saying no more often than not. It won't feel good at first, and it may *never* feel good to you, but this is part of developing leadership discipline.

You should treat your calendar in a similar fashion. Look at each entry, look at the sheet on the wall, and then ask yourself, *Why is this here? Do I need to be doing this? Where in this schedule will I carve out time to focus on my big priorities?*

Like most of the topics covered in this book, time management may be more or less important to you *right now* than it was ten years ago or will be ten years from now. If you are convinced that you are managing your time effectively, your people are doing the same, and you and they are allocating time wisely to your organization's most important priorities, and thereby serving as effective role models for your employees, then you should move on with confidence to chapter 3.

On the other hand, if this issue resonates with you, then take additional time to think about it. Spend more time doing one or more of the various exercises suggested in this chapter.

The subsequent chapters of this book introduce issues and responsibilities that will require conscious commitments of your time. Therefore, you will need to have a grip on this area in order to make available the time required to undertake these responsibilities and become a more effective leader.

Suggested Follow-up Steps

1. Track your time for two weeks and break down the results into major categories.

2. Compare how this breakdown matches or is mismatched versus your three to five key priorities. Make a list of the

matches and mismatches. Regarding the mismatches, write down those time allocations that are 2s and 3s and could therefore be performed by others—or should not be performed at all.

3. Create an action plan for dealing with the mismatches. For example, commit to delegating those tasks that could just as easily be performed by someone else. Decide, in advance, to say no to certain time requests that do not fit your key priorities.

4. After a few months, repeat the preceding three steps. Assess whether you are doing a better job of spending your time on critical priorities.

5. Encourage your subordinates to perform these same steps.

3

Giving and Getting Feedback

Effective Leaders Coach Their People and
Actively Seek Coaching Themselves

> **Do you coach and actively develop your key people?**
>
> **Is your feedback specific, timely, and actionable?**
>
> **Do you solicit actionable feedback from your key subordinates?**
>
> **Do you cultivate advisers who are able to confront you with criticisms that you may not want to hear?**

Most executives assert that talent development is critical to the success of their organization. While this is certainly true, in reality many companies and their leaders often perform poorly on this crucial task. The failure usually boils down to a few key issues. First of all, *coaching* and *evaluation* frequently get confused. Many executives use the year-end evaluation process as the first occasion to "coach" their subordinates. At the same time, the evaluation process is typically so time-consuming that true coaching—which should have been done earlier in the year—gets put off and/or pushed out, and the recipient may consequently arrive at year-end feeling surprised, confused, and frustrated. Another challenge is that despite all the discussion of the need to give feedback, many executives aren't very good at it and are, as a result, uncomfortable giving it in a timely, constructive, and actionable fashion.

To compound this problem, as an executive becomes more senior, he or she may feel that there are no longer viable potential coaches from whom to solicit advice. Their superiors (if any) are no longer closely observing their performance. As a result, these leaders may in fact be even more starved for feedback than their own subordinates.

Take Ownership of the Coaching Challenge

Effective feedback and talent evaluation are critical parts of performance management—and ultimately, of achieving your vision. This topic is discussed extensively in business schools, executive training programs, and the popular business press. There's good reason for all this focus: the success of most businesses depends on attracting, retaining, and developing talented people, as well as managing them to achieve key organizational objectives. In order to accomplish this, you need to put in place effective processes for coaching and evaluating your people.

Companies understand that they have to evaluate their people, and most have created systems to do this. Many fewer companies, however, have placed sufficient emphasis on *coaching* their people—intensively focusing on helping them get better and accelerating their development. A portion of this chapter will focus on tackling that key issue.

Later in this chapter, we'll consider how an executive should go about *getting* feedback. While most executives know they are supposed to give their employees coaching, many fewer realize that they also need to take proactive steps to *receive* it. In other words, I'm arguing that they need to "own" the task of going out and getting feedback regarding their performance. Many executives are uncertain and passive about doing this.

In addition to the above topics, we will discuss what constitutes effective feedback. We will explore how to spot and overcome the obstacles to being an effective coach. We will address how critical it is for executives at all levels to develop effective junior coaches—and how to go about doing this. Last, this chapter will review specific approaches to creating a culture of ownership and learning, so that everyone (at junior as well as senior levels) understands that it's their job to get feedback, and their responsibility to overcome the kinds of obstacles that prevent effective feedback from taking place.

Feedback as One of Your Powerful Management Levers

Let's say you've done a good job articulating a clear vision with associated priorities. Next, you've allocated your time so that you can focus on these crucial priorities, and you've encouraged your people to do the same. How does giving feedback fit into this sequence of activities? *Feedback is one of your most powerful levers in managing people to execute those priorities*. Feedback is a critical vehicle for reinforcing priorities and creating align-ment to help achieve the organization's mission.

Coaching, as I define it, is the process of identifying two or three specific strengths and two or three specific weaknesses in the recipient, and then identifying exercises, action steps, and follow-up activities that will help the recipient address the weaknesses and build on the strengths. The weaknesses need to be *specific* and *actionable*, as opposed to vague or amorphous. Further, the actionable advice should be focused, whenever possible, on the recipient's addressable (and objectively observ-able) skills, versus personal characteristics that the recipient might not practically be able to alter.

Effective coaching typically requires either direct observa-tion of the recipient (in the workplace) or detailed questioning of their colleagues, in order to gather sufficient information regarding the recipient. It is best delivered in a setting and at a time (i.e., early enough in the year) in which the receiver is receptive to hearing it and has time to act on it.

Coaching Versus Mentoring

When I discuss this subject with executives, I often discover that there is real confusion about the difference between *coaching* and *mentoring*. As I see it, mentoring involves giving counseling and, sometimes, career advice to the recipient. It doesn't neces-sarily require direct observation or questioning of colleagues on the part of the mentor. Mentors can often do their job by asking the recipient key questions and then reacting to what they hear.

Is mentoring highly critical and important? It absolutely is. It can help the recipient get a better grip on his or her passions and career aspirations, and help identify appropriate tactics for reaching his or her goals. Mentors tend to be older and more experienced, and are therefore in a good position to offer guidance to younger people.

Mentoring, though, is *not* the same as coaching and cannot take its place. Mentoring, done well, takes time. Coaching, done well, often requires substantially *more* time: more work, firsthand observation, and more insight. It is also likely to involve some greater degree of confrontation and accountability on the part of both parties. Typically, it is an iterative process that requires follow-up by the coach and the recipient. It requires very specific, constructive, and actionable communication, versus more vague generalities and observations.

Let me illustrate with a specific case. The CEO of a large, global diversified conglomerate organized an off-site for his senior leadership team in order to discuss a number of strategic challenges their firm was facing. His goal for the session was to systematically discuss these issues and then agree on an overall game plan for addressing them. He asked me to attend and facilitate this session.

In the course of the morning session, the group discussed its most significant frustrations. Several mentioned that the company had a surprisingly high failure rate among its young and middle-level executives. They couldn't figure out why this was the case. They pointed out that they had a very extensive and "sophisticated" year-end review process. In addition, they had a buddy system in the company, whereby junior professionals were paired with senior people, usually from another business unit. They were convinced that this buddy system was a great mechanism for giving career advice and other mentoring to young executives.

I asked the group for more details about how young and midlevel executives were getting coached. They repeated the summary of the company's evaluation process and buddy system. I probed further: "How does someone learn what they're doing right, what they need to improve on, and what steps they need to take to make those improvements?"

"Well," one executive replied, "that naturally *happens*, informally. I had several coaches myself when I was growing up in the company. They were extremely helpful to me."

I persisted: "Are executives rewarded for their coaching prowess? Is it a question on the annual performance review form? How do you know that coaching is actually taking place?"

On this point, no one was quite sure. They each thought it was valued, but admitted that they might want to do some homework on this question. They decided to ask some follow-up questions of mid- and junior-level leaders around the company to get more insight on this issue. A subgroup agreed to report back to the CEO with their findings.

I circled back to the company a couple of weeks later. After investigating these questions, the subgroup found that actual coaching (versus mentoring and year-end evaluation) was at best sporadic. If you were lucky enough to work for a boss who took an interest in coaching you—as certain senior leaders had been, earlier in their careers—then you got coached.

They also observed that some executives were excellent coaches, with a track record of producing disproportionately high numbers of subordinates who eventually became successful midlevel and senior executives. Conversely, they also found that many of their executives were not good coaches, and that spot surveys of younger employees suggested many of them felt they were not getting actively coached. In addition, while there was training for many tasks in the company, there was no formal training on how to coach people. Upon reflection, the subgroup recommended to the CEO that coaching be upgraded as a priority in the company.

How, specifically, did they accomplish this? First, they added an explicit question about coaching in the annual performance review process for executives. In addition, they started a company-sponsored "coaching network," whereby successful coaches could meet, blog, and otherwise share their coaching methods with colleagues. In his speeches and employee meetings, the CEO began talking frequently and forcefully about the importance of good coaching, thereby raising awareness of the issue. Finally, he made sure that he and his senior leadership team were spending more of their own time coaching subordinates. The CEO was an excellent coach, and his active involvement—which was widely noticed—served as another signal of the importance of the activity.

I check back with him on a periodic basis, and he tells me that, thanks in large part to the emphasis on improved coaching processes, they are doing a far better job at cultivating and retaining their promising young executives. He strongly believes, moreover, that this effort is improving company performance.

Typical Impediments to Giving Feedback

All of this may sound fairly straightforward. Coaching is important. Identifying weaknesses, and working on overcoming them, is how individuals and organizations get better. Seems obvious, yes? If that's true, why don't up-and-coming managers, as well as senior leaders, coach more, and coach more effectively? Why, even in the best of companies, does the frequency and quality of coaching typically rate very low in employee surveys?

One reason is that leaders at many of those companies fail to distinguish between *coaching* and *year-end evaluation*. I think this is an unanticipated and unfortunate outcome of a heightened interest in evaluation in recent years. For example, many companies have adopted some version of a *360-degree feedback* review process, whereby an individual gets feedback from multiple directions: subordinates, peers, supervisors, even customers and vendors. Most organizations use this tool primarily for year-end review purposes and other individual appraisals.

Yes, 360-degree reviews and similar tools have their place in a bigger developmental system. Many leaders, though, mistakenly believe that the year-end review is the most appropriate time to also coach the recipient. After all (they reason), the data has been gathered, the reviewer is well prepared, and a specific time has been scheduled. In addition, so many hours have been spent by senior professionals filling out reviews on numerous recipients that these senior people are often worn out by the process. They feel that if they're spending so much time in late summer and fall filling out reviews, they can't see allocating any additional time during the year to giving feedback. *So*—they reason—*let's just do the feedback at the same time we do the year-end review!*

In most cases, this is a mistake. The year-end review typically represents a sort of "verdict" for the recipient. It happens far too late in the year for these subordinates to take actions that will influence their compensation, review rating, and/or promotion prospects. They know this, and they are in a poor frame of mind to receive and process constructive feedback, or to develop action steps that would help them make improvements. They are often nervous and defensive. In many cases, they're aware that their families are at home waiting for a phone call with a full report as soon as it's "over."

Again, it's as if the jury has come in with its decision, at which point it is far too late for constructive criticism or do-overs. If in that year-end review the employee hears feedback that comes as a surprise, he or she is likely to feel upset, angry, and even betrayed by the reviewer—who, typically, is his or her boss. In my experience, subordinates who get blindsided in a year-end review take that turn of events very, very seriously. The relationship of trust and communication that needs to exist in any effective working relationship may be irreparably damaged. The blindsided subordinate may lose faith in the organization, get demotivated, and become more open to taking a phone call from a headhunter. The ultimate and unwelcome result is sometimes the "surprise" departure of that subordinate from the organization.

The upshot: coaching is something that must occur during the year, well in advance of the year-end review. It should be done early enough in the year that the recipient has time to act on the information and work to make improvements, so that he or she can positively affect his or her year-end performance evaluation review.

No Surprises

A good rule I've always tried to follow is "no surprises" in year-end performance reviews. In other words, if the first time

I have presented a constructive criticism to a subordinate is in his or her year-end review, then *I* have screwed up. Observing this rule helps remind me to stay on top of subordinates' performances during the year and then proactively coach those subordinates based on those assessments. In turn, it also helps subordinates feel more confident that they work in an environment that is *fair*—and while they may not always like the feedback they get, they can be confident that it's intended to help them learn and grow.

Many best practices are developed from stressful experiences. Certainly, many of my most stressful experiences at Goldman Sachs occurred in connection with the biannual round of partner promotions. I had many superb subordinates who desperately wanted to be promoted to partnership. The process at Goldman was highly competitive, with an abundance of talented candidates. Many candidates had attractive offers from other firms, but decided to stay on at Goldman because of the firm's culture, its commitment to excellence, and—very importantly—the prospect that they would be promoted. Probably the most difficult thing I had to do as a manager at Goldman was to tell a superb candidate that he or she was *not* going to be promoted that year and would have to wait until sometime in the future. This was often met with anger, and sometimes even expressions of betrayal, depending on the specifics of the situation.

Because of the searing nature of these discussions, I learned that it was absolutely critical that professionals be coached early in the year, well before the year-end review process. This coaching happened several times during the year and took the form of a very candid assessment in which we discussed their strengths, weaknesses, and potential actions for remediation. The more blunt and frequent these discussions, the better. As a result, if a candidate was disappointed, I could refer back to coaching discussions we'd been having during the year, which had helped inform the current promotion decision. The coaching history also helped retain the candidate at the firm by laying the foundation for what he or she needed to do to get promoted in the future.

These promotion experiences, tough as they were, taught me that you are unlikely to be able to give each of your subordinates all that they might want. You *can*, however, help each of them improve and be their best. I learned that if you have aggressively and transparently worked to coach them, you have a dramatically better chance of seeing them improve their performance, keeping their respect and trust in the face of bad news, and having them stay at the firm.

It Takes Time to Prepare

A second reason why managers fail to engage in successful coaching is that coaching, done right, takes a lot of preparation—which takes a meaningful amount of time. One of the most important leadership lessons for young, newly minted managers is understanding the amount of time that is required to properly prepare in order to effectively coach key subordinates.

I often hear from executives that they "don't have time to coach people." But can that really be true? Presumably, one of your most important jobs as a leader is attracting, retaining, and developing talent. If so, you need to carve out the time needed to focus on this priority. Think about the time management issues raised in the last chapter. What are you do-ing *instead* of coaching that is far less important than coaching? (Get that less important activity off your plate.) If you are un-able to coach your direct reports, you probably have too many direct reports.

It's hard to overstress this point: *coaching is central to your job as a leader*. Many organizations fail to hold on to key talent because their leaders come up short as coaches.

As noted, coaching requires direct observation and/or in-terviewing key colleagues to gather information about the coaching recipient. A leader has to make time for this. While boards of directors may find it necessary to contract out the information-gathering part of CEO coaching—a subject to which we'll return shortly—a manager should really do this process himself for his direct reports. Contributions from outside coaches may go part of the way toward getting the job done, but they really don't discharge your obligations as a leader. Your subordinates want to get *your* feedback. They want to know what *you* think, based on your personal observa-tions and conversations with their colleagues. After all: you set their compensation, and you decide whether or not they will be promoted. They need, and deserve, *your* feedback. Many other tasks can be delegated, but not this one. Make the time.

Fear of Confrontation

Another reason why coaching in the organizational setting is so often inadequate is that *coaching requires a willingness to con-front*. Some leaders perform the necessary observations, collect the relevant data, and develop a clear picture of the weaknesses of key subordinates. Yet they can't bring themselves to communicate those weaknesses and suggest corrective action until circumstances force their hand—most often, when they have to explain why the employee isn't being promoted, or is receiving an unwelcome compensation surprise, or (in the most extreme case) is getting fired. Right up until that moment, the subordinate may well have liked and respected the senior person. After that point, most likely, he or she is furious and has stopped trusting and respecting the more senior colleague.

Are you fearful that giving constructive feedback will cause a subordinate to dislike you? Would you rather be loved right up to the moment that the employee gets the bad news, and then despised—or consistently respected? Are you somehow afraid that giving feedback will demoralize the subordinate? What is holding you back?

I can honestly say that I have seldom seen a subordinate leave a company because he or she was coached too much—as long as the coaching was done in a constructive manner. On the other hand, I have seen many subordinates leave because they felt they didn't get honest feedback during the year, and stopped trusting the firm's senior people.

Where did they go? For the most part, they sought out a new place where they could learn and be coached. They didn't go looking for a place that would be easier or less confrontational. They sought out an organization whose leaders would act in a straightforward and challenging way, rather than tiptoeing around key issues. In these organizations, senior people earned their subordinates' respect and trust by helping them face reality.

A young executive who was attending Harvard for an executive leadership class had recently taken over the reins of a mid-size business unit at a large industrial company. Having heard me give a talk regarding the importance of direct and blunt coaching, she sought me out.

"I don't think I can give people bad news," she began. "I can't tell them that they need to improve in certain areas."

"Why not?" I asked.

"I don't really know," she replied, obviously troubled. "Maybe I just fear confrontation. Maybe I don't have enough experience in this job. Also, I don't like to upset people. Maybe I want too much to be liked?" She went on to say that her relationships with several of her key subordinates had already been damaged because she couldn't bear to confront them with coaching, and instead had surprised them at year-end with a negative compensation message. Several accused her of being "passive-aggressive." Truthfully—she admitted—she was scared, and confused about how to deliver effective feedback.

I gave her several kinds of advice. First, I suggested that her overwhelming desire to be liked and her fear of confrontation might have deep-seated roots. I encouraged her to reflect on her life experiences and try to think about why she feared confrontation. If she had a "support team" of close friends and family members, this might be a fruitful subject to discuss with them. I also suggested that if she thought it would be helpful, consulting a psychologist or psychiatrist might be a very positive move, and might help her to better understand herself in this area.

Perhaps you're surprised to learn of a business school professor encouraging a practicing manager to consult a mental health professional. Don't be. The fact is, many of the biggest impediments to effective leadership lie within. Whatever you can do to confront and deal with your own inner fears and demons is likely to make you more effective. If there's help out there to be had, avail yourself of it.

Second, I underscored the point that *no one* enjoys giving negative feedback. To reduce the stress and overcome her fears, I recommended "overpreparing" for the coaching session. This might include, for example, extensive interviews with colleagues of the recipient. It might include thinking about her delivery, perhaps even practicing in front of a mirror. It might include role-playing the coaching session with a trusted colleague—a rehearsal, in effect. Finally, I encouraged her to keep asking herself the tough questions that had been implied by the angry reactions of her subordinates: Do I really want to be thought of as passive-aggressive? Am I really being "nice" by withholding the kinds of information that people need to improve their performance?

She reported back to me several weeks later. She took very seriously my preparation and rehearsal advice. She had just had what she described as a productive coaching session with one of her key people. At its completion, she began to realize, to her surprise, that she might have the potential to eventually "get good at coaching." She also began to understand, moreover, that very few people are born natural coaches, and that development of good coaching skills requires hard work, preparation, and practice.

How Do You Develop a Learning/ Coaching Environment?

If you're convinced that coaching is a critically important function—at least as important as sales skills, financial skills, communication skills, strategy skills, and the like—then the next question is, how can your company train its senior leaders to become more effective coaches?

I can point to four key elements.

Preparation and Incentives

Coaching takes time. Your managers need to know that you believe it is important that they take the time during the year to be up to speed on the strengths and weaknesses of their direct reports, discuss with their subordinates what they can do better and actions to address those issues, and follow up on a regular basis to monitor progress and give additional advice.

Excellent companies view being a great coach as a criterion for promotion to higher managerial levels, as well as an important determinant of compensation. Think about the feedback you're giving your key managers regarding the importance of their being a good coach in your overall assessment of their job performance.

Specific, Actionable Feedback and Proposed Remedies

Effective feedback should be very specific and focused on skills. It should be *actionable*. It should avoid veering off into the ad hominem (that is, a personal attack), and it should steer away from being amorphous and vague. Similarly, the follow-up remediation advice needs to be specific and actionable.

To illustrate with a bad example: one piece of advice that professionals often hear is that they need to "raise their profile" in the company. Honestly, I have no idea what this means. This type of vague advice often comes from a coach who has "impressions" of the recipient but hasn't done the homework necessary to give the subordinate actionable feedback. This kind of amorphous advice is confusing. Worse, it may actually distract the recipient from confronting the two or three skill-based weaknesses he or she really does need to address.

Similarly, telling someone that they acted "stupidly" is not very helpful feedback if they're trying to dissect what they should have done, and determine what they might need to do differently in the future. It risks insulting and upsetting them, without giving them enough specifics to chart a clear path forward.

Again—specific, clear, and actionable!

Updating and Follow-up

No company would adopt an organizational strategy and then fail to update it over the years. The same holds true for coaching. In a very real sense, coaching is an effort to help drive the specifics of an individual strategy—it demands updating and follow-up.

The needs of the organization change. The dreams of employees also change. Subordinates not only want to be coached on how to succeed in their current job, but also want to develop skills that will help them step up to their next assignment. In order for you to coach effectively, therefore, it helps to have a view on what that next assignment might be so you can help the subordinate develop accordingly.

For example, a great salesperson may want to become a sales manager. To reach this aspiration, he or she will want to be challenged enough today to develop the skills necessary to be ready when the sales manager opportunity arises. What's the vision for the subordinate's future, and how will we get there and on what schedule? What coaching and job assignments might make sense to help that person get there? How and when can we check in to gauge progress against that plan?

Creating a Culture of Ownership

As a leader, you want it to be everyone's job to give feedback and seek out feedback.

Who is responsible in an organization for feedback? I used to tell every new class of Goldman Sachs associates that it was *100 percent* the subordinates' job to seek out feedback—to know their key strengths and weaknesses, and determine action steps to address those weaknesses. At the same time, I regularly told every group of managers that it was *100 percent* their job to give feedback to subordinates.

Was I trying to be funny? Was I trying to have it both ways? No. My point was, and is, that junior people have to "own" the challenge of seeking feedback, and senior people have to own the challenge of giving it. Only if both sides have this attitude are you going to create a true learning environment in which effective coaching will occur. In this type of environment, every employee is invested in development, there are no victims, and people can be confident that they will have the opportunity to grow, learn, and develop.

The ultimate goal can't be that everyone gets promoted or reaches the top level of compensation. Instead, the goal should be that each professional is afforded the *opportunity* to reach his or her potential. It is worth striving to create the kind of culture in which this can happen. This might include, for example, celebrating great coaches, telling "war stories" about how people got developed in the company, and applauding someone who has made significant progress toward a self-improvement goal as a result of seeking out and receiving effective coaching. Because these types of leadership "shout-outs" and anecdotes tend to get circulated all over the company and take on a life of their own, they can help you make the desired point in a powerful and far-reaching way.

When a company is failing to achieve its goals, that failure can often be traced to having inadequate people in one or more key positions. That deficiency, in turn, can often be traced back to the inability of the enterprise to attract, retain, and develop key people. Dig deeper, and you may find a lack of emphasis on coaching and creating a learning atmosphere in the company. It is no accident that great *coaching* cultures tend to be a magnet for outstanding people. Give yourself that great competitive advantage.

Getting Feedback

It's lonely at the top.

We've all heard the expression—so often, in fact, that it hardly even registers in our minds anymore. Randy Newman wrote a song about it. Sooner or later, most U.S. presidents talk about it.

Speaking personally, I never really understood what *lonely at the top* meant until I ran a big business. As I became more senior and took on greater responsibilities, I found that people started to treat me a bit nicer, complimented me more effusively, and became much more careful about what they said when they came into my office.

At first, I felt a little flattered. Over time, I realized they were tiptoeing around me in a way they hadn't done before. I learned that I had to make a much greater effort to avoid getting out of touch. During my last three years at the firm, when I sat on the chief executive office floor, I noticed that there was less people traffic, it was a lot quieter than I was accustomed to, and when people came to our floor, they were a bit intimidated and on their best behavior. I realized that it had suddenly gotten much, much easier for me to get out of touch with reality.

The phrase gained additional resonance for me over the years as I advised leaders who ran large organizations. A real phenomenon of isolation tends to beset the leader, with potentially serious consequences for both the leader and the organization.

By the time you get to "the top," you no doubt have honed a set of skills that enable you to be effective at a number of key elements of your job. Unfortunately, unless you take specific corrective actions, you are likely to become ever more isolated from bad news. You are likely to hear far less constructive feedback about your own performance (at least until it becomes a major problem). You may unintentionally give off a vibe that you really don't want to hear bad news—particularly, bad news about you. As you become more senior and "important," your people may become less and less likely to *want* to give you news that you may not want to hear.

If you sit on an executive floor that is isolated from your operating divisions, this problem is likely to be exacerbated. This phenomenon happens frequently to people who visit the White House. Even if they disagree vehemently with one or more of the current president's policies, once they step into that Oval Office, they tend to be positive and avoid provoking an unpleasant exchange. They are understandably intimidated by the rarified surroundings and the grandeur of the office. They are eager to have a positive exchange and leave the president with a good impression, as opposed to pressing key points that might be unwelcome.

An analogous circumstance arises in business. Lots of people are willing to complain to their colleagues about the CEO, and talk about what the CEO is doing wrong and should be doing differently. Ironically, many of those same people turn to mush when given the opportunity to speak up directly to the CEO. Why? They want the CEO to have a positive impression of them, and not making waves seems like the safe "default" approach. As a consequence, the leader is often the last to hear constructive criticisms that may be circulating widely throughout the organization.

I argue, therefore, that the leader has to take specific steps, go the extra mile—and sometimes, to extraordinary lengths—to get the feedback that he or she needs.

Receiving Downward Feedback

By the time you are the head of an organization or a major unit within an organization, you probably are spending very little time with folks who are senior to you. Your superiors are certainly not observing you firsthand on a regular basis. If you *are* spending time with them, it is typically not in the kinds of settings where they can observe you performing various aspects of your job. Instead, it's more likely a case of you listening to them, or of you presenting to them in some type of meeting. The setting, most often, is a conference room. Most often, there's an agenda to be followed. Very little occurs in the way of unscripted exchange. They don't watch you conduct business and interact with your subordinates or customers. Your superiors, therefore, are not likely to learn much about you in that context. Worse, if you're a very articulate and polished presenter—as you probably are at this point in your career—your seniors may make assumptions about your other skills that are quite inaccurate.

The result? Most likely, the limited feedback that they give you is based on information from your colleagues, your year-end evaluation, and the impressions they get of you in the kinds of structured settings described above. Information they hear in the gossip and rumor mills may also come into play.

You are now in more or less the same situation that I described earlier in the chapter, in which the subordinate doesn't get the feedback that he or she needs until it's too late. By the time your superior or your board "discovers" issues about your performance, it is probably after these issues have metastasized into major problems. As a result, there may be less chance for you to address that problem, and a correctable weakness that could have been easily rectified can have real and negative repercussions for you and your career.

Many boards don't have a firm grip on the strengths and weaknesses of their CEOs. The CEO may be a terrific presenter and may be very persuasive and charming in relation to board members. But these political skills may only mask some of the kinds of performance issues that often come with being "the leader." Those boards that *don't* have an effective process for truly understanding their CEO may find that they have few options when the company runs into operating trouble, has compliance issues, or begins to lose key executives.

For this reason, many boards insist on a 360-degree review process so that they become better informed about their CEO's relative strengths and weaknesses. Sometimes CEOs confide in me that they find this process threatening; I tell them to get over it. This kind of process, done right, can help board members realize the CEO needs coaching and specific help. Rather than shortening the career of a CEO, it can prolong it.

A Board Can Take Greater Ownership of Coaching Its CEO

The CEO of a large industrial company had just led the enterprise through the toughest months of the economic crisis, and had made a number of key strategic choices that served as the basis for a dramatic restructuring of the business. The board was quite pleased with the CEO and very supportive of his actions.

At the same time, several of the board members were hearing (directly and indirectly) significant negative feedback regarding the "leadership style" of the CEO. For example, a key customer of the firm reached out to a specific board member to say that their account coverage person had complained about a severe deterioration in the culture of the company. They went on to say that the word on the street was that the CEO was domineering, had developed a "crony" system among senior leaders, and was a very poor listener. Other board members had heard similar feedback outside the company. A few others had been approached by senior company executives who also wanted to complain (off the record) about the leadership style of the CEO.

The board did not have in place a 360-degree feedback process for the CEO. They did conduct an annual review of his performance, which focused on his success at achieving certain key operating and strategic metrics—return on equity, stock price performance, market share data, and several others. The CEO did not have a coach and instead had identified two board members as his "mentors." These board members tried to act as a sounding board for the CEO and, toward that end, had dinner with him once every quarter.

This situation posed a real dilemma for the board. The board asked me to give them advice at their next regularly scheduled meeting. At this board meeting, we discussed the limitations of "mentoring" and the fact that the CEO really needed a coach. This would not be easy, because the board couldn't observe him on a daily basis and there was not a system in place that collected feedback on him. They didn't want to do anything to undermine the CEO, and yet they also were keenly aware of their obligation to coach him, as well as to ultimately evaluate his overall performance.

For starters, in the very near term, they agreed that they wanted him to get coaching. After all, he was a first-time chief executive, and it was understandable that he needed to get more feedback regarding how to develop his leadership style. He needed to hear this feedback in an organized way and then take steps to work on the relevant issues that came to light.

After the meeting, the board raised the issue with the CEO. They mutually agreed to hire an outside coach who would work with him. They wisely decided to separate the coaching process from the CEO evaluation process. It was agreed that, for this first year, the feedback from the coach would be strictly for developmental purposes rather than for performance evaluation. They also agreed that, in the subsequent year, they would install a 360-degree review system that would give the board information they could incorporate into the executive's year-end evaluation/review.

Two weeks later, they selected an excellent outside coach, and he proceeded to have his first meeting with the CEO. After this meeting, the coach interviewed twenty or so key employees who interacted frequently with the executive. Each participant was assured that his or her feedback would be taken on a confidential, "no names" basis. After gathering the feedback, the outside coach then reviewed it with the CEO and then, separately, with the chairman of the board plus two other board members who had been selected to be part of this process.

The feedback highlighted a number of management style issues that the CEO agreed he needed to work on. (He appeared not to resent the comments, although he admitted that he was surprised by a number of them.) The coach worked with him on action steps to address these issues, and the three board members also gave their advice on actions the CEO might take to address these issues. All in all, it proved to be a very constructive process, and the CEO was highly motivated to improve in the highlighted areas. He realized that he needed to do a better job being in touch with his people in order to solicit feedback more proactively.

The board, too, changed its ways. In retrospect, they realized that they had not focused enough on coaching and that the relatively unstructured mentoring process that had been set up with the CEO was insufficient. In light of this experience, they realized the vital importance putting a coaching process in place.

Proactively Taking Steps to Receive Upward Feedback

As described earlier, it's difficult to get top-down feedback at senior levels, mainly because your superiors get so little exposure to you. On the other hand, unless you are truly isolated, a number of your key subordinates get the opportunity to see you in action on a regular basis. If they are a diverse group, they are likely to have a wide range of opinions regarding your weaknesses. Most likely, they also have ideas about the kinds of remedial actions that you should take to address those weaknesses.

Some people find this notion threatening—the idea that there is a group of subordinates out there with a bead on their shortcomings as leaders—but I encourage you to think of this group as one of your greatest resources.

The problem, of course, is that while these folks represent an enormous reservoir of potentially valuable feedback, you have to take proactive steps to get that feedback early and often. Otherwise, the first time you hear it may be in your year-end review, which is based on their 360-degree feedback. (Too late!) Unless your subordinates have a professional death wish, they are quite unlikely to want to confront you with constructive criticism. As a result, one of your challenges is to find ways to get that feedback—probably through soliciting it (or prying it out of them) in an appropriate manner. Outstanding executives learn how to have these conversations and get this valuable feedback.

In my experience, this is not an easy task, at least initially. First of all, it needs to be done one-on-one, versus in a group. Junior people are not going to be open in their criticisms of you in front of others. In a one-on-one meeting, you have the best chance to convince the person to level with you. Even in a one-on-one, it will take some practice to learn how to elicit helpful comments.

When I first ask a subordinate for constructive feedback, they tend to begin by telling me that I'm doing "very well" on all fronts. When I follow up and ask, "Well, what should I be doing differently?" they respond, "Nothing that I can think of." If I challenge them by saying, "Hey—there must be something!" still they tend to say, "No, really; nothing comes to mind."

I then ask them to sit back and think a little more. "We have plenty of time," I say. An awkward silence tends to ensue. Beads of sweat start appearing on their forehead. They are probably thinking, "Oh, my lord, this guy is really *serious*—what the heck am I supposed to say now?"

At that point, in some cases, they look like they're about to speak, and then stop themselves. I then usually have to ask, "What were you about to say? Please go on and say it!"

At this moment, they typically throw out something that they've been thinking but have been afraid to say. That "something" is often devastating—because it is a fundamental criticism, because I know it's accurate, and because I realize that many people in the organization probably have the same observation.

Ouch! If you have ever gone through this process yourself, you know that you need to maintain your composure, sincerely thank that person for their feedback, and then call a close friend or loved one to ask whether this criticism sounds accurate. Most likely, they will pause and say, "Well, yes, that *does* sound like you."

OK, so you now have an agenda item to work on. You need to take steps to address this weakness—which you almost certainly can do if you are open to improving yourself. The good news is that in my experience, I find that 90 percent of the battle is getting the feedback. Once you realize that you have a specific weakness, you can almost certainly find ways to address it and improve.

Sometime after this interaction, make a point of seeking out that brave truth-telling subordinate, thank them, and communicate that you are working on steps to address the weakness that they identified. Furthermore, tell the subordinate that you might like to follow up with them in the future to get their feedback regarding whether they believe that you've made progress. This will be highly motivating to the subordinate, who will realize that they have had a real influence on the company. Most likely, that story and its aftermath will circulate around the company through word of mouth. In the future, that junior person (and others like them) may be willing to come to your office and give you advice, if they see something that you might be able to do better. This, too, gets around the company.

You're not doing this to be popular or to be "seen" to be asking for advice. You're doing it because it gives you an early warning system for improving your performance. Having seen this experience repeated numerous times—and having been through it myself—I offer the following advice: cultivate a group of individual subordinate coaches with whom you meet one-on-one on some regular schedule to solicit honest feedback. Almost certainly, you will need to convince them that you *truly want* this feedback, and that they are more likely to advance their careers by flagging issues and problems to you than by only giving you "happy talk."

If you *act* on their advice, assuming it's on target and appropriate, this will reinforce their behavior and send a strong message to others that you are a leader who wants to hear the truth in order to improve yourself and the business. If you are sincere about receiving constructive criticism, and highly motivated to continue learning and improving, subordinates and colleagues will gravitate toward wanting to help you.

When this culture develops, subordinates help you identify and address issues before they become damaging to your company or your career. They help you, personally, adapt to changes in the environment, and they help you identify areas in which the company may be out of alignment and therefore vulnerable. You become a lot less lonely at the top.

Of course, this approach requires you to be open to learning, adapting, and hearing constructive feedback. It requires you to keep your ego in check, and to suppress the very human impulse to conclude—now that you're in that corner office—that you no longer need to learn anything.

Trust me: you do. We *all* do.

A Culture of Learning

As an executive and an adviser, I have always been interested why certain companies in an industry succeed and others fail—or at least, perform at a lower level of success. Often, they have the same strategies, hire the same caliber of people, and exhibit other similarities. I believe that one key difference is what they do with their talented people once they join the firm.

In the most successful enterprises, there is a culture of learning, in which all professionals, regardless of level, are doing their best to improve and ultimately reach their true potential. The leaders of these enterprises help make this happen by setting expectations, providing training, and challenging each professional to take ownership of getting coaching—and at the same time, challenging those same professionals to take ownership of *giving* coaching. Executives in these organizations seem to be better than their peers at producing leaders, minimizing unwanted turnover, and getting the most from their scarce people resources.

How you answer and act on the questions posed at the outset of this chapter will go a long way in determining whether your organization has the skills necessary to achieve its vision and accomplish key priorities. That's also why, in terms of your time management, this is one area that *you* must make space for. While some coaching processes can be delegated to others, responsibility for coaching your direct reports falls on you—you own it!

In the next chapter, we will take this a step further. A critical precondition to effective succession planning, and its resulting benefits, is the development of strong talent development processes and a culture of coaching. Success in this area will help ensure that you are developing a pipeline of outstanding talent to fill key leadership jobs, which in turn will be essential to your own success as a leader of your organization.

Suggested Follow-up Steps

1. For each of your direct reports, write down three to five specific strengths. In addition, write down at least two or three specific skills or tasks that you believe they could improve on in order to improve their performance and advance their careers. Allocate time to directly observing their performance, and discreetly make inquiries to gather information and insights in order to prepare this analysis.

2. Schedule time with each subordinate, at least six months in advance of the year-end review, to discuss your observations and identify specific action steps that could help

them improve and address their developmental needs and opportunities.

3. Write down a realistic list of your own strengths and weaknesses. Make a list of at least five subordinates from whom you could solicit feedback regarding your strengths and weaknesses. Meet with each subordinate individually and explain that you need their help. In your meetings, make sure to ask them to give you advice regarding at least one or two tasks or skills they believe you could improve on. Thank them for their help.

4. Write down an action plan for addressing your own weaknesses and developmental needs. If you have a direct superior (or trusted peer), consider soliciting advice regarding your developmental needs and potential action steps. Depending on your situation and level in the organization, consider the option of hiring an outside coach.

5. Encourage each of your direct reports to follow these same steps regarding their direct reports and themselves.

4

Succession Planning and Delegation

Owning the Challenge of Developing
Successors in Your Organization

Do you have a succession-planning process for key positions?

Have you identified potential successors for your job?

If not, what is stopping you?

Do you delegate sufficiently?

Have you become a decision-making bottleneck?

One of the critical roles of a leader is "getting the right people in the right seats." Put another way, attracting, retaining, and developing talented people—and appropriately deploying them in important positions—is vital to the success of most organizations. If you're going to achieve your vision and execute major priorities at a high level of excellence, you need to have developed the talent necessary to get the job done.

Succession planning, combined with effective evaluation and coaching programs, is the next critical task you must undertake in order to build your organization and succeed in your own job. Let me sharpen this point a step further: an essential responsibility of an outstanding leader is to develop potential successors for key positions. *You must own this responsibility.*

Failure to Develop Successors Often Leads to Broader Issues

Most of the business leaders I speak with nod their heads enthusiastically when I talk about this priority. A few have given me some combination of a nod and a shrug, perhaps implying that this strikes them as self-evident: *of course I believe that attracting, retaining, and developing people is important!*

And yet, when I dig a little deeper, it turns out that many of these same leaders have not set up a succession plan for key positions within their company. They fail to recognize that many of the "burning issues" they have come to speak with me about ultimately relate to their failure to develop potential successors in general and for their *own* job in particular. This failure typically creates a series of other problems in their organizations, which are symptomatic of their deficiencies in managing talent. So why don't these executives see this issue more clearly and press themselves harder to upgrade their performance in this area? As with a number of other straightforward concepts in this book, it is a lot easier to talk about than to accomplish.

A Road Map

In this chapter, we will look at the critical importance of succession planning and the related issue of effective delegation. We will discuss the real costs of failing to develop appropriate successors. In my experience, if you haven't identified potential successors for key jobs—including *your* job—it is very likely that you are also not delegating sufficiently and are probably a significant bottleneck for key decisions. As a result, you may be experiencing real constraints in your ability to run your business unit or build a superb company.

Outstanding people tend to abandon a work environment in which they believe they are not being groomed for greater responsibility through a well-planned series of key job assignments and effective coaching. The loss of these high-potential people is the functional equivalent of throwing large sums of money (think stacks of $1,000 bills) out the window of your office—not something you would knowingly do!

You'll notice that in this chapter, I will discuss succession planning first and delegation second. Why? In order to achieve your vision and top priorities, you need to delegate several critical tasks. The succession-planning process helps inform your thinking about the individuals to whom you should be delegating. You need to decide *to whom* you're going to assign responsibilities before you actually start to delegate.

Too often, leaders give up on delegating because, initially, it doesn't seem to go very well. This is usually because they have not first identified their best talent, and *then* matched key assignments with capabilities and development aspirations of those talented individuals. These leaders don't see the connection between succession planning and delegation.

Once executives embrace the idea of succession planning and implement an effective process, they more confidently embrace the idea of delegating much more extensively and effectively. In addition, they tend to follow up this delegation with much more targeted coaching and advice. They also begin to connect achieving their own aspirations with doing a better job of succession planning and delegation.

This is not necessarily an easy road to follow. There are several impediments and red flags to be wary of and to work to counteract. We'll explore some of these issues in the next several pages.

Danger Sign: A Leadership "Team of Cronies"

Historian Doris Kearns Goodwin described Abraham Lincoln's cabinet as a "team of rivals" and explored the tensions and outcomes associated with Lincoln's courageous (and sometimes counterintuitive) leadership style.[1] Many executives have taken note of and learned from this historical example of strong leadership. On the other hand, all too often, corporate leaders take a different path and fall into the trap of assembling a "team of cronies."

Why would they make *that* choice? Many leaders have spent years getting into their current job, and they certainly don't want to give it up. Consciously or unconsciously, they think of talented subordinates as an eventual threat to their own job. In these cases, the leaders know intellectually that the

organization will be stronger if they develop potential successors, but a deep-seated insecurity overwhelms this intellectual
understanding.

Unfortunately, I've observed several companies in which
the leaders are determined to keep their job for as long as possible, and have absolutely no desire to truly develop diverse
talent that could potentially threaten them. In some cases, surprisingly, these leaders are the CEOs; in other cases, they are
younger business unit heads who hope to someday become
CEO. These people tend to have some degree of insecurity
about their current jobs, and they certainly don't want to take
any actions that might make them feel even *more* insecure.
They may make a show of *talking about* succession planning
and talent development. They may even implement some sort
of succession process, but on a consistent basis, they promote
key lieutenants who are loyal to them personally, with whom
they've worked previously, and who share viewpoints very
similar to their own. If they are challenged about this pattern,
they carefully explain that other seemingly more talented subordinates are simply not as good as the folks they have chosen.

And so they hunker down and dig in. They give off a powerful "do not enter" vibe to highly talented subordinates and
colleagues who are not part of their clique. Unfortunately, the
result is that they often (intentionally or unintentionally) drive
away key talent from the organization; create leadership teams
that are loyal to them *personally*, rather than to the company;
and develop debilitating blind spots and judgment gaps due to
the collective deficiencies of their senior leadership team.

It normally takes a crisis of some kind to highlight these
judgment gaps. By the time the crisis occurs, it may be too late

to fix the situation and lure back desperately needed talent that has long since departed. As a result, the company may suffer severe and long-term damage.

In a public company, it's the job of senior leadership and, ultimately, the board of directors to monitor for this type of issue and to ensure that transparent succession processes take place. Regular job rotations—aimed at breaking up cliques, among other good outcomes—are also helpful in this regard. But *most* helpful is avoiding cliques and cronyism in the first place, by cultivating leaders who are committed to cultivating *more* great leaders based on merit and an openness to diverse points of view.

"We Just Don't Have Enough Talented People!"

I often meet with leaders who are struggling to match their time with their key priorities. They are doing too much by themselves, working constantly, and can't seem to focus on the key issues facing the company. When I ask why they aren't delegating some of their less critical tasks to promising subordinates, they respond that they would love to, but unfortunately, their company has a "shortage of talent." Typically, the CEO or business unit leader then goes on to explain how difficult it has been to attract, retain, and develop critical talent.

This is a dangerous and unhealthy situation for all parties involved—and it's potentially *most* damaging to the leader who is in charge. If you are in this position—if you can't find talented subordinates to whom you can hand off significant managerial responsibilities—then one of two things is likely to be true:

1. Your perception is correct. There is a talent deficit in your organization.

2. Your perception is incorrect. There's no lack of talent in your organization, but you aren't using it effectively.

In the first case, you need to address the situation immediately—in other words, go out and interview and hire key talent. You also need to determine why your organization is not developing better-quality talent within. Is there a problem with entry-level recruiting? Are you losing talented recruits before they get seasoned enough to become leaders? Is there a problem with the career development and skill development processes in your company? Are you and your senior leaders failing to track the best talent in the organization or failing to attend to their job assignments, career trajectory, and coaching needs?

As you're doing this, you also need to keep in mind that the second explanation might also be correct. Perhaps you need to look in the mirror and figure out whether you (among others) are simply not recognizing and valuing resident talent. Is it sitting there right under your nose?

A major division head of a large company was concerned about what she perceived to be a talent deficit in her organization. She felt that she could not use her time to the fullest, because she viewed her direct reports as incapable of assuming some of her major responsibilities. She also believed that this talent deficit was keeping the company from launching several new product and market initiatives. She pulled out her "depth chart" of talent, which detailed all her direct reports, as well as their direct reports. I went through the names with her and asked her about the suitability of several of the executives for greater responsibility. She was complimentary of several, but still conveyed a certain measure of ambivalence about each of them.

As our conversations continued over the next three months, two of the subordinates whom we had been discussing quit. Each left to assume increased responsibilities at a major competitor. In both cases, the division leader (with help from the CEO) tried furiously to persuade the departing individual to stay, emphasizing that she was actively considering that person for a significant new leadership assignment. Unfortunately, neither of the departing executives believed her. They had seen no evidence up to that point that they were being groomed or coached for increased responsibilities and were therefore justifiably skeptical about the eleventh hour retention pitch. As a consequence, each decided to leave the firm.

In the wake of their departures, the division leader was truly devastated, and her CEO was openly expressing concerns about this executive's ability to attract and retain key talent. In other words, an already challenging situation had just gotten far worse. This trauma was sufficient to cause the division head to seek advice, and motivate her to do some productive reflection and analysis. As we talked through what had just happened, she realized that, prior to the defections, she really had not identified these individuals (or anyone else) as high-potential leaders. As a result, she failed to put increased responsibilities in their hands and did not actively ratchet up her coaching of them. She admitted that in the crush of daily events and the strain of keeping up with the business, she hadn't carved out the time to truly get to know them and accurately assess their potential. She realized now that she had underestimated the capabilities of these two employees—and that she was probably underestimating the abilities of several others in her division.

I encouraged her to sit down and make a list of potential "stars" in the division. She then blocked out time to spend with each of them individually. Prior to these meetings, she pulled out their personnel files in order to read their historical performance reviews, job assignment histories, and backgrounds. In the meetings with these individuals, she asked several questions to make sure her "picture" of them was up to date, and also encouraged them to talk about their career aspirations and goals.

As a result of all this, she worked out a career and responsibility game plan for each person. She used this plan, in turn, to create a draft succession plan for the top positions in her division. While she was quite heartened by this process, she also candidly admitted that she probably had waited far too long to undertake this exercise. On a positive note, she subsequently presented this succession plan to the company's CEO, who was so impressed that he suggested the methodology be rolled out across the entire firm.

Succession Planning: A Leadership Tool

In most cases, there *is* a nucleus of talent in the organization—but it may not have been fully tapped into. A well-developed succession-planning process can be an extremely helpful discipline in identifying that pool of talent, assessing it, and then matching it with key needs of the business. The process leads to asking a number of very constructive questions, starting with, "Is there someone here who can take my place?" If the answer is no, the next question is, "Should I hire a search firm to look outside the company, in order to recruit the caliber of talent that could eventually take my job?"

If the answer to that first question is yes—there *are* potential successors—then the next questions should be, "Am I spending enough time understanding these people's aspirations and generally getting to know them better? Should I be delegating more mindfully to each talented person, raising my expectations of them, and coaching them more intensively, so I can develop them more rapidly at the same time that I'm testing their capabilities? Do I need to move one or more of them into the first of a planned series of key assignments to help develop their skills?[2]

If you decide to do this, not only will the subordinates' performance improve, but *your own* performance will improve, as well. As you're making things explicit and comprehensible to each individual, key priorities are likely to be performed at a much higher level. You're raising the bar both for that person and for yourself, because the teacher always learns something from the talented student.

Hopefully, you have spotted at least two or three people in the organization who are potential successors to you. You don't need to inform them explicitly that they are "successors," but if you follow a plan of giving them more responsibility and coaching, those two or three promising younger people are likely to contribute more to the organization and be even more motivated to do their best. By so doing, they will dramatically improve your ability to perform at your best.

Think back to what I said earlier about some senior people being overly anxious about developing potential successors who could inadvertently hasten their own departure. In most cases, that scenario simply doesn't play out. If you perform better, your organization will perform better, and your tenure and longevity are more likely to be extended.

Stated another way, you, as a leader, should be more concerned about the scenario in which you *don't* develop successors. Great companies reward business unit leaders who develop talented subordinates who can eventually take their place. Conversely, they are reluctant to promote business unit leaders who, given sufficient time in their jobs, fail to develop talented subordinates into potential successors.

The Responsibility of Every Leader

During my career at Goldman Sachs, we put *enormous* effort into attracting, retaining, and developing talent. I was taught that succession is a critical responsibility of every leader, and I communicated that to each of my direct reports. We had a well-developed succession-planning process, and we had regular career development discussions that focused on job assignments, career potential, and the coaching needs of up-and-coming talent. When we set out to fill leadership openings, we almost always began with a review of internal candidates. When we identified a great internal candidate for a bigger job, we simultaneously discussed who might take that person's place if and when we promoted them.

On occasion, we would discover that the candidate in question had not developed a subordinate who was capable of taking his or her place. When that proved to be the case, we would dig a bit to see why this was so. If we found this person had a history of failing to develop subordinates, then that was often sufficient reason *not* to promote them. Why would we want to put someone in a bigger job, with even more at stake, when that person hadn't been able to develop talent in his or her current position?

When someone was denied a promotion for this reason, it tended to make a searing impression on that individual. It also helped reinforce the corporate culture, which was underpinned by the conviction that developing talent is a central contributor to building a stronger, more successful firm!

A Benefit of a Strong Succession Process: Creating One Firm

A clear succession process helps teach executives how to think about developing talent. It gives senior leadership the opportunity to coach the next level of leadership on this subject and also assess the company's talent on an organization-wide basis.

For example: if a business unit leader, after honestly appraising his talent pool, believes he has a shortage of talent, he needs to initiate a plan to search within the company—or, if necessary, outside the company—in order to build a reserve of talent. Conversely, if a business unit leader has a surplus of potential successors, one or more of these folks can be transferred to leadership jobs in another part of the company as those jobs open up. This process helps ensure that great potential executives don't get "trapped" in a particular business unit, and that the entire company gets the benefit of talent development.

In strong companies, there are invariably certain leaders who consistently develop great talent. If you examine how they accomplish this, you're likely to find that they are good recruiters, good coaches, and extremely thoughtful about how they assign jobs to their best people. You're also likely to find that these people think of the organization first and of themselves second. They overcome their own insecurities and put their energy into making their organization better. In my experience, great companies and nonprofits are almost always built around these types of people. They should be rewarded, promoted, and held up as role models within the enterprise.

How to Develop a Succession-Planning Culture

Let's get more concrete about how you and your company can develop a culture based on effective succession planning. I'll point to four specific actions you can take; most likely, you and your colleagues will discover other steps that are relevant to your particular circumstances.

Create a Depth Chart

As discussed earlier, this can be very simple and straightforward. The relevant business unit leaders (including you) should list the key job positions that report directly to them. For each of these positions, the business leader should create a corresponding list of those people who, within a reasonable period of time, could credibly do the job. For each candidate, it is helpful to have up-to-date biographical information; an assessment of strengths, weaknesses, and developmental needs; and a summary of expressed career aspirations. This analysis should be updated and then reviewed by company leadership on an annual or semiannual basis. A typical outcome of these reviews is the creation of a developmental action plan for each candidate as well as other steps, which might include a decision to recruit additional talent from outside the company.

There's no one format that a depth chart needs to follow. Much depends on the size and complexity of your organization. I've seen a depth chart that was two sides of a single sheet. I've also been in a large windowless room at the corporate headquarters of a mid-western consumer goods giant that had a map of the world covering three of its four walls, with little tags representing hundreds of managers at all ranks, color-coded to indicate function, education, skill sets, expressed career path interests, and so on. The executives referred to this room as the "war room." Whenever a job above a certain level looked as if it might soon be opening up, a senior team unlocked the door to the war room, went inside, and began examining tags, with a view to moving them on this board.

This might be overkill for all but the biggest companies, but you see the point: the depth chart is something to take very seriously. You should ask each of your business unit leaders to own this process of analysis for their specific areas of responsibility. This topic should be an established part of your regular business review sessions with direct reports. Effective execution of this effort will help ensure effective development and deployment of your people, and should be a vital contributor to your sustained success.

Devise a Career Development Plan

You should come up with a career development plan for each potential successor to a key job in the organization. This plan should detail who will "own" this person's career by serving as his or her coach (and potentially asking for the help of others to also help coach the person), as well as a list of potential job assignments that would help develop this individual. This could be some combination of a new business unit, functional, and/or geographic assignment.

These plans need to be discussed and updated on a regular basis. This should not be a pro forma exercise, and plans should not be allowed to get stale. It should be the responsibility of each business unit leader to update this plan for each of his or her direct reports.

Review and Follow Up

Hold succession planning meetings with your key business unit leaders on a semi-annual or annual basis. Follow up to be sure coaching responsibilities are being fulfilled well in advance of the year-end review—see chapter 3—so that the recipient has plenty of time and an action plan to work on his or her weaknesses and development needs. A well-thought-out series of job assignments should be updated, with a view toward developing the person for greater responsibility.

Make sure that developing key talent is an evaluation element in the year-end reviews, compensation, and promotion processes at your organization.

Be a Role Model for Talent Development

Make sure you are serving as a role model for this activity. Some significant portion of your time should be spent on identifying talent, coaching key people, and crafting thoughtful job assignments for your direct reports.

Think about how you can make your commitment *visible*. Make sure you are participating in important succession-planning and talent review meetings. Yes, this is important work in and of itself. In addition, your good work in succession planning is critical as a teaching tool. It sends an important message across the organization about the importance of talent development.

The leadership group of a very successful global industrial company did an excellent job executing the various elements of succession planning. Among his other roles, the CEO viewed himself as the "chief talent officer" for the company. He believed that talent was a vital competitive advantage they had to develop in order to achieve their objective of being a leader in each of their major businesses units and making a positive impact on the world. He consciously allocated a full 20 percent of his time to attracting, retaining, and developing key talent. He believed that the company could *never* have enough talent, and he felt it was healthy to "run scared" when it came to finding, developing, and retaining great people.

The company's succession-planning processes were quite sophisticated and dovetailed with the organization's coaching, review, and training processes. The CEO openly described himself as being an "enemy of cliques." He declared that he wanted the company to embody "diversity," in the broadest sense. In other words, he wanted not only racial and gender diversity, but also a diversity of thought and perspectives.

While he had close professional relationships with his direct reports, he didn't allow himself to become their "buddy" outside of work. As he explained to me, he questioned the wisdom of leaders socializing and becoming too friendly with key subordinates. He feared that this type of socializing might send a signal that an executive had to be a personal friend of the CEO in order to get promoted. In one memorable conversation, he told me that he didn't want his key reports laughing at his jokes if they weren't funny. "And the fact is," he deadpanned, "I'm not that funny."

When I talked to other executives in the company, it became clear that they deeply respected the CEO and felt a strong loyalty to him. When pressed about why, one senior executive expressed views that I heard from several others: "I believe it is fair here. I know I will be judged on the merits of what I do. The CEO judges me on the basis of the work I do, and not on my personal relationship with him. We have well-developed processes that give me great confidence that I will be challenged, coached, and given assignments that will give me the chance to show what I can do.

"I'm loyal to this company. I know the CEO will do what's best for the company. I have confidence that what's best for this company will ultimately be best for me—and that I will reach my potential here."

Wow! And as noted above, this was not unique; in fact, these views cascaded through the company. There was widespread acknowledgment of the need for alternative points of view, disagreements, different backgrounds, and overall fairness, including assessments based on professional performance rather than personal relationships. All in all, it was an impressive example of a group of self-confident leaders running an impressive company.

The Importance of Delegating: How Succession Planning Can Bridge the Divide

Once you have developed processes to identify potential successors and key emerging talent, you will know to whom you want to delegate key tasks.

As discussed earlier, the failure to identify appropriate successors almost always goes hand in hand with the unwillingness or inability to delegate sufficiently. Whenever I meet a leader who is overworked and feels that his or her organization is not reaching its potential, I know that I am likely to discover that he or she is spending excessive amounts of time on various noncritical tasks and *not* spending sufficient time on his or her highest priorities.

For example: The CEO of a large private business based in Latin America was visiting Harvard to speak to students. On the trip, he dropped by my office to catch up. He started the conversation by remarking how thrilled he was to escape his company even for just a few hours. He appeared quite stressed and frustrated. Like so many other firms, his company had suffered serious setbacks during the recent economic crisis. It had been an ordeal, professionally and personally, and he told me that he felt "just plain tired."

He explained that he truly wanted to delegate X, Y, and Z, but really didn't think he had key leaders to whom he would feel confident in delegating. "I'm fighting a lot of fires," he told me. "I know you emphasize spending time on key priorities, Rob, but you don't understand—I don't have the bandwidth to spend more time with customers, drive other key initiatives, or coach my key subordinates. Also, my kids are complaining that I'm never around, and my wife is losing patience with me. I guess you could say that I'm feeling trapped . . . maybe *suffocated* would be a better description."

We proceeded to explore a number of the ideas discussed in previous chapters. What were his aspirations for the company? What three to five priorities were most critical to the achievement of those aspirations?

This was as far as we progressed in this meeting, because he realized that he hadn't thought extensively about these questions in several years, and the economic crisis had probably also altered his views on these questions. "Interesting," he said, without prompting from me. "I suppose I should have been regularly spending a portion of my time thinking about vision and priorities—and, when times got *really bad*, I should have been thinking about this even more."

We met again a few weeks later. After he laid out his revised priorities—which were well thought out and compelling—we then identified and discussed the mismatches between those key priorities and how he was spending his time. We then went through, name by name, a list of the key leaders in the company. A number of them had excellent educational credentials, and several had strong records of professional accomplishments at their previous firms.

With his permission, I then met with several of these leaders over the ensuing few weeks. I also further studied their backgrounds and looked at the results of their year-end performance reviews. Armed with this information, I sat down again with the CEO. Together, we looked at the jobs that each individual currently held, and explored what kinds of new or added responsibilities might fit their talents and passions. I urged the CEO to have an open mind as we conducted this discussion: nothing should be ruled in, but nothing should be ruled out.

On the basis of all these discussions, we were able to identify a series of tasks that could be transferred from the CEO to one or more of these individuals. The transfers would include periodic progress reviews on the part of the CEO—both to make sure that the subordinates had the tools, backup, and coaching that they needed, and to give the CEO some additional peace of mind about delegating what he perceived to be key responsibilities.

Needless to say, the executives involved reacted very favorably to their increased responsibilities. They felt more valued by their boss—and by extension, their company. They were genuinely pleased that the CEO was learning to leverage their skills and, consequently, further develop himself. They were also relieved that the CEO was now able to spend more time on the company's most urgent priorities.

Of course, almost none of this was "easy," especially the implementation phase. I checked in periodically with this particular CEO and found that, on occasion, he reverted back to his old ways—injecting himself into situations where he really wasn't needed. We agreed that he had to practice "counting to ten" before he plunged into these matters. The result of this pause was that, more often than not, he stopped himself from getting involved.

This CEO discovered not only that he could learn to delegate successfully, but also that many of the delegated tasks were now being done far more effectively than if he had performed them himself. (His subordinates had the *time* to do the job, and—in many cases—they had more talent and experience than he did, in these specific areas.) He now spent much more time on strategy, key customer cultivation, and coaching—and got home for dinner most nights.

Leadership Is a Team Sport

Unfortunately, this is an all-too-common tale. I have heard it told countless times—unhappy stories of leaders who just can't seem to find sufficient time to spend on key tasks that are vital to their company. Why is this so? Maybe, they haven't identified key talent through succession-planning processes? Are they delegating to that talent? Are they coaching that talent?

If the answer to any of these questions is no, they have to ask themselves why. This may require facing their insecurities and idiosyncrasies. They will likely have to challenge themselves to get more comfortable with "giving up some control"—which I would rephrase as "sharing responsibility."

Leadership is a team sport. Let's extend the sports analogy. A great golfer is a solo operator. So is a great tennis player (at least in singles), and so is a great bowler. Running an organization, by contrast, is a team sport. In team sports, the best individual player is highly unlikely to play well enough by himself or herself to help their team beat an excellent opponent that operates as an integrated team.

So you have to ask yourself, *what sport am I playing?* As a senior leader, you know you must assemble a group that has the requisite skills and has been delegated (by you) the appropriate responsibilities to accomplish key tasks and priorities. If you have the mind-set of a professional golfer as you step out onto a football field, you are very likely to get clobbered. Why in the world would you lead your organization in a manner that is going to get you clobbered?

The Subtle Bottleneck

Maybe you have done all the steps recommended above. Maybe you have identified key tasks to delegate, identified appropriate talent, and delegated responsibilities to key subordinates.

Yet, somehow, you can't seem to get out from under those responsibilities. They keep coming back at you. They just can't seem to get addressed without your involvement.

The CEO of a real estate firm headquartered in Europe was attending a class at Harvard Business School. He came to visit me after participating in a case discussion that highlighted the importance of succession planning and delegation. After we discussed the strategy options for his company, he explained to me that "delegation" really hadn't worked well for him. He described how he regularly got "pulled back" into all sorts of different decisions that he had delegated to others, and professed to be somewhat annoyed about this. He asked me whether I might visit his company when I was next in Europe, and meet with a few of his senior leaders.

I did this a couple of months later. During these meetings, it became clear that while the CEO did delegate, he seldom stood behind the subordinates to whom he delegated. When subordinates came to him asking for help on a delegated task, rather than saying no and redirecting the person back to the executive to whom the task had been delegated, he was often inclined to say yes, even though this had the immediate effect of nullifying the delegation and confusing the executive who was supposed to be responsible for the task at hand.

He also had a bad habit of second-guessing the decisions made by his subordinates, even when those decisions really were not sufficiently material to have an impact on the ultimate progress of the organization. Rather than "picking his spots" for disagreeing, he tended to be undisciplined. The intermediate-term result of this lack of discipline was that those executives to whom he had notionally delegated responsibility started coming to him to get his check-off—even on minor decisions. Gradually, word got around the company, and more and more people started showing up on his doorstep. "It saves time," they explained to me, "because I know he's going to want to weigh in, anyway." Worst of all, when the CEO was unavailable, routine decisions got held up as people waited for him to surface.

Meanwhile, the company was facing a number of strategic challenges that the CEO did not seem to have time to address. I found that several key senior people were actively thinking about leaving because they felt it was "rudderless."

I confronted the CEO with what I observed. We talked extensively about this, and he commented that it drove him crazy that certain tasks done by others were just not done as well as if he did them himself. He acknowledged that he intellectually understood that all tasks did not need to be performed optimally. Equally, he understood that unless he stopped being a bottleneck, started backing up his people, and stopped second-guessing his subordinates, the company was heading for trouble in terms of its strategic positioning and direction. Well before that, it was also likely to start losing its best people.

I visited the company six months later and found that he had worked hard to make significant progress in this area. It did not come naturally, but he was now motivated to address this issue and improve.

Learning to Pick Your Spots

Does any part of this story sound like you? Do you bristle at the thought of even minor tasks being done less well by others than you could do them yourself? If so, fix it. Agreeing to take on tasks that you've already delegated—or second-guessing your subordinates excessively—will turn you into a bottleneck and take you away from doing the tasks that should constitute your *real* job.

If you truly want to delegate, make sure you back up those key executives to whom you delegate responsibility. Intervene only when the task at hand is of sufficient importance to merit your involvement. When you are inclined to intervene, make sure you have discussed that decision *in advance* with the executive involved.

To summarize, consider saying something like the following to your executive: "You decide about X, Y, and Z—I don't need to weigh in at all. Please check with me on A, B, and C. Otherwise, I am, of course, here if you want my opinion, but I am happy for you to check with me only when it's helpful to you." As noted, avoid second-guessing your people unless there is a heck of a good reason to do so—and then be prepared to engage in damage control.

How Long Is Your Shadow?

Leaders cast a shadow. You may not see the shadow, but your people do.

The CEO of a privately held company on the West Coast was known as a pioneer in his industry and had accomplished a great deal. He was in his early sixties and was the majority stockholder in the company. He was justifiably concerned about what would happen to his firm when he was no longer in a position to run it.

He explained to me that he had been very generous with compensation and felt he had a superb group of talented people. I knew that he was generally acknowledged to be a good spotter and recruiter of talent, and he was extremely clear about delegating key responsibilities and backing up that delegation. Just one problem: despite doing many of the things I talk about in this chapter, he was quite uncertain whether the company would someday be able to function effectively without his presence. Over the previous five years, he had hired a number of excellent leaders, with proven management and leadership experience, in order to bolster the potential reserve of talent that could ultimately take his place in the future. I met a number of these executives and was quite favorably impressed.

So why was he so unsure about succession? What was the problem? *Was* there a problem? After I spent more time with him and other key company leaders, one thing became clear: he just *couldn't refrain* from butting in and asserting himself in the organization. He couldn't let the enormously competent people with whom he had surrounded himself do their jobs.

So yes, there was a problem: he was so highly respected in the company that even a little tap on the shoulder from him felt (to many of his subordinates) like an anvil dropped on their heads. These people *so badly* wanted to make sure he was happy with them. As one relatively high-ranking executive put it, "He casts a really long shadow." Hmm.

How long is *your* shadow? If you started your firm and are the patriarch or matriarch, be aware that you may need to take key steps to *shorten* that shadow. This involves recognizing that your subordinates may not do tasks as well as you or the same way you would—but that does not mean that they won't do them quite effectively. Allowing them to do so will train them, build your bench, and free you to focus on those tasks that the organization desperately needs you to attend to.

Skating into the Future

Wayne Gretzky, perhaps the greatest hockey player of all time, has been widely quoted as saying that his challenge was not to skate to where the puck was, but instead, to anticipate where the puck was *going to be*, and skate to that point. In this same way, leaders need to build their organizations to compete in a dynamic marketplace. They need to anticipate where the world is going.

Superb leaders know that, no matter how talented they are, they can't do this alone. They know they need to assemble a diverse group of talented people, develop those people in a dynamic manner that fits their skills and aspirations, and put them in key positions so they can contribute to the organization. I strongly believe that the earlier in their career young leaders develop this mind-set, the more successful they are likely to become.

Succession planning is a critical part of the process of identifying and then developing critical talent. Strong companies develop firm-wide succession-planning processes that help executives at all levels learn how to effectively identify and nurture key talent. This is particularly useful to newly minted managers, who might be unaccustomed to identifying and developing talent as well as working through others.

Using succession-planning processes, business unit leaders can thoughtfully delegate key responsibilities to these identified emerging executives, so that the business unit and the organization can build a cadre of capable leaders. Talent pool development and thoughtful delegation have the added benefit of freeing leaders to allocate their time to the most critical challenges facing the business.

As discussed in this chapter, many executives agree with the need to delegate but often need convincing regarding succession planning. I hope this chapter helps convince you of the direct connection between these two activities. It will be more difficult to achieve your vision and key priorities—and to reserve the bandwidth you need to perform the other tasks that *you* must own—without having first built a competence in this vital area.

Suggested Follow-up Steps

1. Create a succession-planning depth chart for your business unit or organization (as described earlier in this chapter).

This document should include at least two or three potential successors for your own position.

2. For each potential successor, write down their key development needs and specific actions you might take in order to develop their capabilities in relation to potential future positions. Work to develop and shape these specific development plans. Make use of the developmental action plans prepared as part of your chapter 3 follow-up steps.

3. For those key tasks that you have committed to finding a way to delegate (see chapter 2), begin matching those tasks with specific candidates on the depth chart. Make assignments.

4. Categorize delegated tasks in terms of their levels of importance to your enterprise. Based on this analysis, note which tasks need to be done at extremely high levels of quality, and which can be done at "sufficient" levels of quality. Ask whether you have calibrated your level of involvement to this categorization, and remember that "involvement" should often take the form of coaching the subordinate, rather than a direct intervention. Make a commitment to "picking your spots," to ensure that your direct interventions (beyond coaching) are justified by an appropriately high level of task importance.

5. Ask your business unit leaders to perform this same exercise with regard to their direct reports.

5

Evaluation and Alignment

The Courage to Assess Your Enterprise
with a Clean Sheet of Paper

> **Is the design of your company still aligned with your vision and priorities?**
>
> **If you had to design the enterprise today with a clean sheet of paper, how would you change the people, key tasks, organizational structure, culture, and your leadership style?**
>
> **Why haven't you made these changes?**
>
> **Have you pushed yourself and your organization to do this clean-sheet-of-paper exercise?**

Many successful businesses and nonprofit organizations go through stretches of time during which they are achieving their most important objectives. Everything seems to be in sync. The organization has the right mix of talented people; it is pursuing market segments in which it has distinctive competencies that it brings to bear effectively; tasks are organized in a manner that is highly effective; the promotion and compensation systems create incentives that reinforce desired behaviors, which in turn lead to achieving major organizational priorities; the culture reinforces critical behaviors that help the organization succeed; the organization's leaders are effective, in terms of their leadership styles, and are widely respected. If it's a business, it is highly profitable and is building an increasingly strong franchise. If it's a nonprofit, it is serving an important social need at a high level of quality. Employee morale and pride are high.

When all these elements come together in this manner, it's great fun, and it's *deeply satisfying* both to employees and to key constituents of the organization. For those of us who are or seek to be leaders, this is the environment and set of circumstances that we strive so hard to create in our organizations.

And then, something changes. It always does.

Sooner or later, inevitably, something happens that upsets this special equilibrium and threatens to throw the organization either modestly or substantially out of alignment. It may not be noticeable until much later, but the seeds of challenge have been planted.

What happens? It could be one of any number of events. The world changes—for example, there's a recession. Leading players in the industry merge. Critical products mature or become commoditized. A competitor unveils a significant technological innovation that threatens the viability of your business model by undermining one or more of your distinctive competencies. A competitor hires away valuable talent that was critical to the company's success. A central member of your team decides to retire.

Or maybe *you* change. You get bored. You become "successful." You stop listening to your subordinates. You get tired of calling on clients and trying to respond rapidly to their ever-changing demands and needs. (Maybe you decide that *you're* always right, and your clients need to learn that!) Maybe you have made a lot of money, and you'd rather spend your time in a different way. For whatever reason, the job is no longer as fun or as meaningful—and this change affects your leadership actions.

I could continue this list indefinitely, cataloging all the kinds of unwelcome changes that might occur inside or outside your company. These changes may negatively affect the organization's culture, undermine its distinctive competencies, change its value proposition to the customer, or simply erode the organization's edge—the edge that has helped it succeed up to now. Whatever the specifics, the bottom line is that *the design of the organization is no longer aligned with achieving its vision and key priorities*. Something needs fixing.

Broken in Menlo Park

A Menlo Park, California–based technology firm had consistently prospered and grown since its founding in the 1980s. Yes, there were plenty of growing pains, but overall, the organization performed extremely well and was very much in alignment with its goal of producing innovative products that served the critical needs of its customers. In addition, over the years, the company built a very high-quality team of professionals, particularly in the research and product development areas.

One reason for the company's success was the truly cutting-edge nature of its flagship product: an integrated hardware/software package that was central to the manufacturing processes of its key customers, most of which were large global manufacturers of industrial products. The company had been originally founded around the development of this product, and had made refinements and built out product adjacencies, over the years, to meet the evolving needs of its customers.

Many of the members of the senior leadership team had started with the company at its inception. The CEO was an excellent recruiter and had done a superb job of identifying highly talented people with several years of engineering and product design experience at other technology firms in Silicon Valley. Being an excellent software engineer and product design expert himself, he personally coached many of these new hires as they came aboard. Also, the CEO spent substantial time with the company's product development engineers, helping them think about customers' needs and brainstorming about better ways to design and upgrade their products.

Over the years, the product design team of approximately fifteen professionals was divided into industry segments, so that the company could better tailor its products to manufacturing processes specific to the various industries it served. As employees became more seasoned at the firm, they often emulated the CEO's behavior, and a culture of coaching and innovation prevailed. An informal buddy system developed, with each senior person taking responsibility for helping an assigned younger colleague succeed.

The company went public in the 1990s, and, by 2006, it was generating annual sales in excess of $2 billion. Over this period, it had built a very impressive record of revenue and profit performance and, more important, had built a strong base of loyal customers.

In 2006, the company launched an innovative new product that was intended to better serve the critical needs of its current customers and also enable the company to sell its product to new industries it hadn't previously served. As a result of the new product introduction, the CEO believed that the company needed to build its sales force and grow its overall headcount to support potential future growth. The board of directors was strongly supportive, the business environment was very positive, and the future looked bright.

Before 2006 was over, though, signs of strain began to emerge. The CEO and his senior people found it increasingly difficult to find time for all the tasks that were necessary to run a bigger firm: training new staff, initiating high-quality coverage of new industry sectors, and servicing the increasing needs of existing customers. Employees of the firm were working increased hours, taking on greater responsibilities, and traveling far more extensively. Despite the greater hours, many commented that they felt as if they were getting less and less accomplished. The CEO observed that certain fundamental mistakes were starting to be made—errors of execution that hadn't been common at the firm previously.

Stress levels continued to rise and morale began to deteriorate. A few key people resigned without much apparent warning. Two went to competing technology start-ups. The CEO noted, with chagrin, that these new start-ups looked a lot like *his* company, back in its earlier days. More ominously, two longtime customers discontinued their purchases of company products and began buying from a competitor. In a meeting with the CEO after informing him of their decision, these customers observed that they felt that the company was no longer as attuned to their needs and now seemed to be more focused on growth than serving its loyal longtime customers. Needless to say, this was a jolt to the CEO and the company.

The firm that had been so rewarding and fun in previous years was now much more challenging. The CEO was concerned about the company's declining stock price, and his thoughts also began to wander to the long-term lease they had just signed on the firm's new headquarters building. Had that been a mistake?

When I first met with the CEO in 2006, he quickly got to the point. "I thought growth was a *good* thing," he said, shaking his head. "Now I'm not so sure. In fact, I think we might have had a better company when we were smaller."

We talked about the firm's trajectory over the past several years. He readily admitted that he wasn't sure they had made the necessary adjustments to accommodate their rapid growth. He wasn't sure that their sales force, in conjunction with the product design team, had sufficient bandwidth to stay attuned to the changing needs of existing customers while at the same time learning to serve entirely new customer segments. In addition, he worried that the company had failed to develop a systematic process for training and coaching new hires—both in product development and in the sales force.

The buddy system worked well when the company was smaller, but had fallen by the wayside in the chaos of the firm's growth. In addition, in the past, the norm had been for the product design group to have regularly scheduled meetings with the sales force, in order to monitor customer needs and new competitive developments; and product people had made it a priority to accompany sales representatives on visits to key customers. With increased travel demands, though, people now often called in by phone—or even missed these interdepartmental meetings altogether—and product development staff visited customers much less frequently.

The CEO had not designated key lieutenants to whom he would increasingly delegate important tasks relating to product design, sales force management, and interdivisional coordination. He also had not designated senior lieutenants to be responsible for new-employee training, investor relations, and certain other significant functions.

I suggested that the CEO should schedule an off-site with his senior leaders. I agreed to facilitate and lead this session. In this off-site, they would step back from their day-to-day activities and determine what processes, people, tasks, and incentives would be necessary to successfully achieve the firm's vision and top priorities. This session would also address how key tasks should be delegated among senior leaders of the firm, and how the CEO might need to change his own activities and leadership style in light of the firm's greater size and ambition. Of course, I could have pointed out that this session probably should have been done before they made several of the strategic decisions relating to growth of the firm—but this was water over the dam, by that point.

The meeting was initially awkward and tense. This was the first time in several years that these executives had gone off-site as a group in order to discuss overarching issues at the company. Also, each executive was unhappy about the trajectory of events at the company. Some privately blamed others at the table, while others worried that they might individually be criticized for some of the difficulties.

After some warm-up exercises intended to help get these people more open to talking and listening, the first issue we discussed at length was the vision and priorities for the firm. As part of this, we talked about whether and how they should grow the firm. Did they want to tackle these new products and industry segments—and if so, why? Should they, instead, simply continue to serve their existing customer base? What should be the criteria for deciding whether to develop a new product or pursue a new market?

They each shared their views and ultimately concluded that for a public company in the highly competitive and fast-changing technology sector, standing pat was not an appropriate strategy; they had to find ways to develop products that fit evolving customer needs and to pursue other avenues of intelligent growth that built on their distinctive competencies in serving customers.

After extensive debate on their core competencies and the appropriate vision for this company, they began to come to a consensus regarding a plan. They decided that the company might have taken its eye off the ball in focusing excessively on "growth," per se. Instead, they felt that the guiding light for their key initiatives should be the aspiration of (1) producing a superb product and (2) understanding and serving their customers' needs while (3) producing sustainable and growing investment returns to the company's shareholders.

To accomplish this, they believed that the company should slow down the planned pace of its new product introductions and new industry initiatives, leaving enough time to (1) train new hires, (2) better phase in new customer coverage, so that they could do a more effective job of developing close relationships with these new customers, and (3) develop other key internal processes that were necessary to scale the business.

Next, they focused on internal organizational changes. For example, one change they discussed was that the sales force should be relocated so that it would be adjacent to the research and product development unit. In addition, the weekly interdepartmental meeting should be reinstated and should be chaired by the CEO (for at least the first six months).

They challenged the CEO to delegate more effectively certain important tasks to senior executives. New-hire recruitment and integration, sales/product design coordination, and other such responsibilities had to be specifically assigned by the CEO. They also went so far as to suggest which assignments should go to which senior executives of the team.

This exercise was an enormously helpful prod to get the CEO and these senior leaders to make the necessary changes. Ironically, many of these suggestions had been raised previously over the past few years but never actively pursued and implemented.

To his credit, the CEO acted on these discussions and made a series of critical decisions that allowed the firm to get back into alignment over the subsequent year. As hoped and expected, these changes also set the stage for the next phase of the company's development.

It Pays to Run a Bit Scared

My brief retelling of this episode in the history of this technology company may make it sound obvious that the firm had gotten out of alignment. In fact, it really wasn't obvious at all.

In real time, from the inside, it is often extremely difficult to see when a business or nonprofit has gotten out of alignment. Many leaders don't realize there's a problem until long after misalignment has set in. Problems can take root, grow, and fester for years before it becomes obvious that there are serious issues that need dealing with. In the meantime, the organization might appear to be performing at a very high level of effectiveness.

Early warning signs often come in the form of decreased employee morale, the departure of key people, rumblings among the client base, egos getting out of hand (sometimes manifested in fancy cars, palatial homes, and other ostentatious ornaments of success), and erosion of the firm's reputation with key constituencies.

Eventually, though, these situations tend to reach a tipping point, after which something happens to make the misalignment painfully clear. This event is often a downturn, competitive action, or other change in the external environment. Unfortunately, by the time the issue is apparent, it may be too late to take corrective action. The Menlo Park technology company wasn't quite at that point, but it certainly was getting there.

In previous chapters, I've stressed the importance of the leader's learning to delegate. But this is one of those tasks that the leader *can't* delegate completely. Effective leaders know that one of their primary responsibilities is to regularly check, and recheck, whether the business is in or out of alignment. On this topic, I like to say that *it pays to run a bit scared*. A healthy paranoia is appropriate when you're exploring whether the key elements of your organization still match your aspirations and priorities.

A Mixed Bag: The Challenge of Addressing Alignment

As a leader, you are ultimately responsible for selecting your key people, formulating critical tasks the firm must do well, and designing your organization's structure and practices. As a result of these important decisions, as well as your leadership style, a culture emerges. An enterprise is in alignment when these design factors lead to achievement of critical company goals and priorities. It is out of alignment when one or more of these design factors detract from achieving key objectives.[1]

Typically, businesses are in alignment in some regards and out of alignment in others, and key parts of the business are almost always in transition from one state to the other (from alignment to misalignment, or vice versa). This is because the world is changing very quickly, and most industries today are extremely competitive.

Leaders *know* this, intellectually. From an emotional standpoint, however, it can be very challenging for a leader to recognize that certain key people, as well as other important elements of the design of the business, need to be changed. This is especially true if the leader is also the founder or has been in charge of the business for a number of years. It very difficult for most mortals to admit, or even *see*, that one of their longtime key executives is now in the wrong job because the demands of that job have changed in a fundamental way. Similarly, it's hard to move aside an executive who has grown a business unit to the point that it's now too big or too complex for him or her to handle. This problem becomes even more challenging if that person is strongly averse to teaming up with another executive who has complementary skills, even if that pairing is likely to improve their success and materially prolong their careers.

Similarly, in many cases, it's also extremely hard to phase out a product that historically has been critical to the success of the company. Yes, you may understand intellectually that if you don't prune the product line, you will continue to divert valuable company resources that should be used elsewhere to build the future of the company. For better or worse, though, we humans develop emotional attachments and strong loyalty—even to aging product lines.

Equally difficult is the challenge of changing a compensation system or other processes that represent "the way it has always been done around here." This can be true even when the leadership team understands that the legacy compensation system is failing to promote employee behaviors that are critical to future success, and failing to sufficiently reward those employees who are essential to that success. This situation often arises in companies that want to dramatically increase the amount of cross-selling between business units, yet have embedded compensation systems that pay their professionals primarily for individual production, rather than team-oriented behaviors.

Making changes risks upsetting longtime employees, family members (if it's a family business), board members, or even the previous CEO, if he or she is still a force in the company. Depending on the situation and your own tolerance for conflict, you might want to avoid offending or appearing insensitive to these various stakeholders.

Most important, making changes may make *you* feel uncomfortable. Like most leaders, you have established patterns of behavior that you'd prefer not to alter, even though you might sense that they're no longer productive.

Possibly you've decided that this isn't the right time to make dramatic changes. You might have rationalized that changing key components of the business will create unintended consequences or be disruptive to routines or relationships, and involve new tasks that feel uncomfortable or are distracting to key employees. Finally, it's possible that the proposed changes will take the *fun* out of several key jobs, perhaps including yours.

Given all these caveats, it's not a surprise that many leaders might say, "All things considered, why don't we wait another six months, and *then* we'll consider making some of these changes?" Or better yet: why do we need to fool around with this at all? "If it ain't broke, why fix it?"

Separate *What* Should Be Done from *How* It Should Be Done

My answer would be as follows: first, you need to ask the question and do the analysis of whether you are, in fact, out of alignment. If the answer is yes, you can then assess the urgency of the situation, figure out what changes might need to be made, and determine the degree of difficulty in and tactics for making those various changes.

You should make every effort, initially, to separate your consideration of *what* should be done from *how* it should be done. By jumping too quickly to the *how*, many executives scare themselves away from actually figuring out *what* needs to be done. They are dissuaded from doing the work because they anticipate (sometimes incorrectly) severe cultural resistance to making changes. As a result, they never insist on asking the key questions to get this process rolling.

After doing the analysis, you will be in a better position to assess which changes would be nice to do but would not be critical to the business, versus those actions that are essential to your continued prosperity and competitive positioning. At that point, you will want to develop a detailed plan of action for how to implement the most critical changes.

Be Proactive: Crises Have "Long Roots"

The main points are that *you should not put this off*, and that *you should do it on a regular basis*. A proactive process will help you forestall and prevent a crisis. Of course, some executives believe that a crisis creates an opportunity to make needed changes. I would argue that a well-run organization doesn't need to wait for a crisis to do what needs to be done. Further, if you wait until the point of crisis, you may well have far fewer viable options for addressing the situation. You also are likely to be forced to consider disruptive and even destructive options, which could have been avoided if you had acted proactively. These more disruptive/destructive options may inflict lasting damage on the enterprise, its people, and its franchise.

Let's look briefly at the well-documented case of Xerox Corporation. Xerox was the dominant photocopier company for many years, with a virtual monopoly in its industry. (You didn't "photocopy" something; you "Xeroxed" it.) The company had an impressive history, of which its employees were both aware and justifiably proud. Because it was organized around a breakthrough product innovation, the Xerox culture was heavily product oriented, as opposed to customer oriented.

For years, the company did so well that it did not worry excessively about new product innovations. Even though it maintained an extensive R&D capability in California—where a number of the original innovations that led to the personal computer, the computer mouse, and other cutting-edge products were conceived—the company wasn't as aggressive as others in getting new ideas out of the laboratory and into the marketplace.

This approach worked very effectively for a long time. Xerox was highly profitable, and its stock was a staple in the portfolios of long-term investors, both individual and institutional.

Then things changed. In the 1980s, competitors, particularly in Japan, developed alternative technologies. The digital revolution began making its way into the imaging realm, upsetting the formerly stable apple carts of proud old companies like Kodak and Xerox. Xerox continued to aggressively sell its product in essentially the same way it always had. By all outward appearances, this strategy continued to work. The fact was, however, that the company was drifting out of alignment. Internally, key executives began to raise concerns about fundamental threats to the franchise.

By the end of the 1990s, the company had begun to lose money and was highly leveraged. People started talking about the impending demise of Xerox—an astounding turn of events, given how dominant the company had been only a few years earlier.

Anne M. Mulcahy, named president in May 2000 and CEO in August of the following year, understood that the company was badly out of alignment and that drastic steps were necessary to save it. This understanding was reinforced by the company's leverage, operating results, and falling stock price. Mulcahy restructured, and fired thousands of employees at a company that previously had been seen as a reliable long-term employer. She brought down debt levels, put more money into R&D, and refocused the company culture on customer needs.

All in all, it was a time of great trauma for Xerox. Mulcahy has commented publicly that the crisis that manifested itself in 2000 actually had "long roots" that had developed over many years. Because of the various actions taken to deal with the crisis, the company survived—and recovered, to a meaningful extent—but its leaders learned a costly lesson. They learned the value of running scared in order to preempt crises from occurring, and of proactively thinking about alignment.[2]

Learning from the Great Recession

Think of the many proud businesses, young and old, that failed during the economic crisis that began in 2007. After the fact, some pundits were quick to observe that many of these management teams were out of touch and had failed in their leadership responsibilities. Ironically, some of these same leaders were celebrated by the same pundits just a few years earlier. Some of these businesses were dangerously overleveraged—even though they didn't appear financially fragile just a few years earlier. Some of these business models were overly dependent on key products in which they no longer had a distinctive competitive advantage. Whatever competitive edge they had enjoyed over the years had clearly eroded, and that erosion accelerated during the economic downturn.

What can we learn from all of these sad tales? I submit that they are, at their heart, stories about *veering out of alignment*, usually over the course of many years. The economic crisis was what lawyers might call the *proximate cause*—the thing that actually pushed them over the cliff edge—but what really got them right up to that cliff edge was a series of gradual shifts that took several years to unfold. In each case, key factors slowly changed without an appropriate evaluation and response in realigning the business.

Business is about *change*. Approaches that work in one era usually don't continue to work in another. The trick and obligation for a leader is to be able to recognize when a business is out of alignment, and then to *do* something about it. We all have the capacity to do this—and we each have the capacity to miss it. Asking the question is the first step.

Driving Alignment

Each of the previous chapters has a bearing on the alignment of your organization. Your leadership style and effectiveness are key contributors to that alignment—or lack thereof.

In this context, the clear articulation of a vision with key priorities is the destination toward which you are always driving. Effective alignment is always measured against your success in achieving these objectives.

Coaching is a critical tool in creating alignment. Top-down coaching helps junior people work to achieve company goals. In addition, when senior people have the benefit of junior coaches, they have a built-in early warning system that can signal when the business is getting out of alignment. Talent management and succession-planning processes help ensure that the right people are being deployed to the most critical tasks, which in turn ensures that the organization is achieving its vision and adapting to critical changes in the environment. Moving key talent across the organization into different job functions and geographic regions every few years also helps get a fresh set of eyes on key company issues and practices. Various company processes—such as Monday morning meetings, off-sites, and strategy sessions—are also critical tools in achieving alignment. Your leadership is the first and last line of defense in this effort.

All of these tools and approaches are critical to enhancing alignment and spotting opportunities to realign. In addition, I suggest you consider another useful alignment tool: the task force.

The Task Force: No Sacred Cows

One highly effective way to help evaluate alignment, and develop viable options to improve it, is to take a group of potential successors from different functions and business units of the firm and ask them to work together as a team.

Give them some version of the following assignment: "If we had to start this business from scratch today, how would we do it?" More specifically, the questions they should pursue might include these:

- Are these the markets we would serve? Are these the products and services we would offer? Are these the people we would hire?

- Would we be organized as we are today, or would we be organized in some other way?

- Is this how we would assess and pay our people? If not, how would we do it differently?

- What are the key tasks we would need to be great at? Are they different from what we do currently?

- Is our current culture the one we would foster? If not, how would it need to change?

- Would the composition of our leadership need to change? How would the talents and leadership styles of our current leaders need to change?

Give them a few weeks to answer these questions. Tell them that there are no sacred cows. Tell them that in the end, you may not sign up for *all* of their recommendations, but you definitely want to hear them, and you will make at least some changes based on their advice. In my experience, you will get some superb suggestions, and this team will highlight issues that you may not have been able to see, possibly because you are, at least somewhat, emotionally tied into your current business design and structure.

Task Force Composition: One Level Down

Why this type of task force, versus a small group composed of you and your most senior executives? In my experience, a management level below the top leadership group is often likely to have a greater emotional distance and objectivity in assessing your situation and calling for specific remedies. They are not as emotionally wedded to what has been done up to now, and may not be as sensitive about challenging some of the sacred cows of the organization. Finally, depending on your seniority and leadership style, one level down might be closer to what's happening at the "point of attack" in your business, and—as a result—bring a fresh and different perspective. Ultimately, you and your senior leadership team will need to take up these issues, but this task force can give you a powerful head start and reality check.

A CEO Can Get out of Touch

The CEO of a financial services company based in a southeastern state decided to run this exercise. He was concerned that because of recent consolidations in his industry, the financial crisis, and other competitive and contextual changes, his company might be losing its ability to effectively compete and succeed in its industry. He told me that he was skeptical about whether a task force was a good idea, stating frankly that he thought that it was far more likely to generate naive and superficial advice than real insights. I persuaded him that the costs and risks were relatively low and that—because there was so little to lose—it was worth a try.

He selected four up-and-coming executives from different parts of the company. This four-person task force went to work and five weeks later came back with some preliminary thoughts that called for substantial changes in the company and its strategy. The CEO was startled at the sheer audacity of the group's recommendations, in light of the fact that he knew each of its members to be a measured and careful professional. He met with them and posed several follow-up questions, which they spent the next few weeks answering.

It was at this point in the process that the CEO asked me back for another round of conversations. First, he confessed to me that he was astonished—even shocked—at some of the task force's suggestions. Implementing them would be traumatic to the company. On the other hand, he admitted, he had studied the group's work carefully and knew that they had raised issues that he simply hadn't seen or really didn't want to see—probably because he was the primary architect of the current business strategy and the firm's design. The ideas dealt head-on with the dramatic changes that had taken place in the needs of their customers and the mix of their businesses. Many of the firm's legacy businesses had become commoditized, and unless the company took advantage of its strong client relationships to cross-sell higher-value-added services, its business was likely to erode. Fortunately, the company had a number of the distinctive competencies and product capabilities necessary to make the recommended changes, but to do so would require a revamping of its vision, key priorities, and organization.

After extensive reflection and discussion, the CEO came to the conclusion that many of these ideas were extremely good ones. Significant changes were needed—but if they moved quickly, they could make these changes in a way that was likely to strengthen their competitive positioning in the industry.

While the CEO embraced many of these suggestions, he was also worried that his rank-and-file employees would be unwilling to embrace them and would resist. To address this concern, he subsequently did some spot checks around the firm and was astonished to find that these seemingly "radical" suggestions had the full support of key players in the company's middle and junior ranks. He had to conclude that he was more out of touch with the views of his employees—especially those who were facing clients every day—than he had ever realized.

This story draws on several of the major themes in our preceding chapters. The CEO was out of touch with his company in part because he had not invested sufficiently in a coaching culture, in which he could call on junior coaches to give him and his senior team feedback. He had not focused sufficiently on succession planning, which would have identified up-and-coming stars with whom he should be in touch on some regular basis. Until he asked this task force to take on its assignment, executives subordinate to him did not feel welcome to express views that were contrary to the ones he expressed. He was a more dominant figure than he realized, and the company had become more top-down than was advisable. As a result of this exercise, he now began to realize that there was a compelling need to bring the company into alignment with changes in its customer base and its industry context.

The "clean sheet of paper" analysis by a task force of your emerging leaders is a way of saying to your people, "I'm ready to hear the truth and also *deal* with that truth. I may not agree with everything you say, but I want to hear contrary views." One compelling benefit of the task force approach is that it is highly motivating for junior people. It helps them learn about the company, gives you a chance to see them in action, and communicates that you are a leader who *listens*. Believe me: word soon gets around the company that you implemented an idea that was generated by a task force of midlevel and junior people. Employees hear, from their peers, that this is a company in which young people can have influence *early in their careers*.

How Often Should I Think About Alignment?

Many executives have asked me whether there is a way to make the whole alignment challenge less disruptive. My answer, suggested earlier, is: "Yes—do it on a regular basis."

Done too infrequently, the analysis of alignment can be quite traumatic. If key questions are left unanswered for too long, getting back into alignment tends to require dramatic changes, which can adversely affect individual employees and even damage the organization. To make a medical analogy, it's a lot more advisable to lose 25 pounds when you are healthy and fit than after you've already suffered a severe heart attack, and other medical complications stand in the way of dealing with your health.

Similarly, I'd argue that the U.S. government would have had an easier time dealing with its huge budget deficit during a period of economic prosperity rather than waiting until an economic crisis and an aftermath of sluggish economic growth: can we really raise taxes or substantially cut government spending when the rate of unemployment is unacceptably high? As a consequence of these arguments, no changes are made, and dealing with government debt gets postponed to a later date, when it is most likely to be even harder to deal with.

One of your jobs as a leader is to anticipate challenges and opportunities that are coming down the road, deal with them in an orderly manner, and help keep the company in alignment. Given that fact, what should your people think when they hear that radical changes need to be made in a hurry? They may think that the world has changed pretty radically in a short period of time, or—more likely—they may well think that you've been asleep at the switch and failed them as a leader.

They have a *right* to think that. Your people are counting on you to be thinking about alignment. They have put their faith in your captaining of the ship and in your ability to keep the organization on course. You need to reward that faith. Use these tools early and often. Depending on the industry, I would suggest doing some type of alignment exercise every six to twelve months, and certainly as part of your annual planning process. Thinking about alignment tends to become contagious, and your example will encourage fellow executives to get in the habit of thinking preemptively about these issues.

Seeing the Bigger Picture

It makes sense to study the moves of competitors through this lens. Assign key staff to watch competitors' actions and consider *why* they're doing what they're doing. What does that particular competitive move do to help that company's state of competitiveness? What do you think they see that is causing them to make certain moves? Are they just dumb, or are they seeing something that you are missing? What is it likely to mean for threats to *your* company's competitive position, in the future?

To avoid getting walled off from the world, read the newspaper, online news services, and relevant trade publications regularly. Do you *really* know what's going on out there? As the leader, you need to be up on current events and trends—even ones that don't seem immediately relevant to your organization—and ask how those trends might wind up changing your world.

A Diversity of Views

One reason why the tools described in this chapter can have such a powerful impact is that they allow a *diversity of views* to come to the fore. Yes, debates and disagreement can be irritating, distracting, and uncomfortable. At the same time, they are extremely good medicine for a healthy organization. They help surface a variety of different types of problems and are likely to point to approaches to deal with those problems.

But what happens if the members of your senior leadership are all from similar backgrounds, with similar views—or worse, if they're all your longtime cronies (as discussed in chapter 4)? Almost certainly, there won't be these kinds of salutary debates and disagreements. As a consequence, your company will be at severe risk of "groupthink," in which issues either do not emerge or aren't properly debated. This syndrome was on display during the recent economic crisis, with lack of diversity (in the broadest sense) at the top of a number of companies leading to monolithic thinking, insulation, and—ultimately—severe damage to (or even the economic failure of) the organization.

It's *your* job, as a leader, to ensure that a true diversity of backgrounds, styles, and views is present in the senior ranks of your company. If you can't figure out how to do this, your board may have to help you do it, by encouraging you to surround yourself with people who aren't necessarily close or "loyal" to you. Yes, of course you want loyalty from your key subordinates, but you also want the composition of this group to be based on merit and on the willingness to engage in open debate and disagreement. You want a senior leadership group that will see the world in a variety of ways, disagree with each other, and—most important—have the courage to tell you the truths you need to hear.

Two True Tests of Leadership

In this book, we have talked about the various roles that an effective leader plays. This chapter comprises two of the most important. The first is the leader as "architect." The architect asks the key questions and is constantly seeking clues in order to determine whether the business is in or out of alignment. This task is neither easy nor obvious, but it is critical to the company's fortunes.

The second role of the leader is being an effective agent of change when it becomes clear that your business has gotten out of alignment. Do you have the wisdom, energy, expertise, and courage to make the necessary changes? Do you have sufficient knowledge and relationships in the organization to be able to develop a cogent action plan for successfully executing key changes? This is where coaching, creating a learning environment, and promoting key people who care first about the organization—versus their own parochial interests—are all critical to successfully implementing change.

However you approach the alignment challenge, the key is *asking the questions* and *doing the analysis*. Your critical stakeholders are counting on you.

Suggested Follow-up Steps

1. Identify a key business unit or function to try out the clean-sheet-of-paper exercise. Create a small task force based on the selected names from the succession-planning depth chart exercise. Attempt to draw professionals from at least two to three different business units and/or functional areas. Give the team a specific assignment, and emphasize that they should assume that there are no sacred cows to be protected. Make clear to them that while you may not follow every piece of their advice, you want their candid views and most likely will implement at least some of their suggestions.

2. Agree on an appropriate time frame. Take into account that this assignment is not in place of doing their day jobs. Make clear that you are available to answer questions or give guidance, but you plan to stay away from this

process in order to avoid influencing their analysis and conclusions.

3. Debrief the group regarding their findings. Also, conduct a post mortem to determine what you and the task force learned from the process of doing this exercise.

4. Develop a specific action plan for implementing at least some (if not all) of the group's recommendations.

6

The Leader as Role Model

Communicating What You
Truly Believe and Value

> **Do you act as a role model?**
> **Do your behaviors match your words?**
> **How do you conduct yourself under pressure?**
> **Is your conduct consistent with your stated values?**

Seated at the helm of an organization, a leader wears many hats and plays many roles.

We've talked about several of those roles in this book: the leader as visionary, coach/mentor, organizational architect, and change agent. In addition, the leader may play the role of the wise captain—the person you trust to guide the ship even when no one is quite sure what the future holds. The leader must also be the visible chief guardian of the organization's reputation, ethical standards, and brand integrity.

In some cases, the leader must also be the healer who gets people to work together, forgive each other, and generally get along. Similarly, the leader can serve as convener: the one person who has the clout to get people in the same room and work together to solve a problem.

In this chapter, we will explore in greater detail one of the most critical roles a leader must play—that is, as a model for others, an example for others to follow. Yes, certainly, the leader can and should tell people what he or she wants them to do. In practice, however, these words do not speak as loudly or forcefully as the example he or she sets by exhibiting (or not exhibiting) the requested behavior. Knowingly or unknowingly, *every leader* plays this role. Some leaders, though, are not sufficiently aware that they serve this purpose in an organization. They believe that because they are the leader, they can play by a different set of rules. They believe that it is reasonable to ask employees to "do as I say, not as I do." In these cases, the leaders' actions fail to match their most carefully articulated top priorities (see chapter 2).

This approach doesn't work for very long, if at all. Yes, to a certain extent, the leader *does* play by different rules, and the people in an organization are generally willing to provide some latitude to a leader in judging his or her behavior. That doesn't change the fundamental fact, however, that the leader is the most powerful role model for the people of an organization. Inevitably, his or her behavior will speak louder than any clever slogan or well-polished speech.

How Others See You

Far more than anyone else in an organization, the leader is observed—*by everyone*. Is her door open or closed? Where does she sit? How is his office decorated (and who paid for it)? Does he barricade himself in his office all day, or does he walk around, and even sometimes sit at the lunch table with the employees and shoot the breeze? Does she have a frown on her face or a smile—and what does that say about what she must be thinking and feeling? Does her body language give off an air of superiority or arrogance, or does it suggest that she respects the employees and really wants to get to know people as individuals? What does he do when he gets in an elevator—does he stand alone and look down, or engage the people around him in a friendly way?

Is she friendlier to those above her in the pecking order than she is to those who report to her—in other words, does her demeanor change, based on the stature of the person with whom she's talking? Is she friendly to people face-to-face but critical of them behind their backs? When things go wrong, does he distance himself from the problem—blaming someone else for it—or does he take responsibility and ownership, even if he wasn't the person primarily at fault? Does his exhibited behavior reinforce or contradict his aspirational rhetoric?

Do any of these situations ring a bell with you? Do you have one set of standards for your speeches and a different set for your behavior? Do you have one set of standards for your behavior when you think people are watching, and a different set for when you think no one is watching? If so, why do you think this is OK?

Let's try a few more questions. Do you have your own parking spot in the employee parking lot? Do you eat in the company cafeteria or in an executive dining room? Do you fly first class even when the rest of your team is back in coach? Do you ask to be reimbursed for first class on relatively short trips, even though company policy states that you are supposed to fly coach class on trips of less than four hours?

Do you live by a set of rules different from those that you ask your people to live by? If so, why? What gives you the idea that you need and deserve "special handling?"

Again, does any of this get you to thinking? What do you do in these and similar types of situations? What do your actions say about who you are and the type of company you want to build? Does your behavior reinforce or contradict the values you espouse, the culture you say you wish to build, and the vision you articulate for the firm? What messages—reinforcing or undermining—are you sending by the way you behave?

Words Versus Actions: Do You Walk the Talk?

The managing partner of a hedge fund had built an excellent firm over several years. He had taken the time at the inception of the firm to write down a detailed set of business principles, which were on the wall of every office, frequently reprinted in company documents, and posted prominently on the corporate Web sites. He even had these principles—which emphasized concepts such as the importance of teamwork, innovation, looking out for each other, and long-term thinking in investment decisions—printed on little laminated cards so that people could carry them in their pockets. Whenever the subject came up in conversation, he said emphatically that he wanted to build a learning environment, in which young people were coached and mentored and could learn from their mistakes.

This was also a key part of his recruiting pitch to every potential new hire: *if this is the kind of culture you want, then you should come work with us.*

In my later talks with this leader and his employees, it became clear that he had adhered to these principles consistently during the first few years of the firm's existence. Once the fund passed several billion dollars under management, the firm was obliged to get bigger, and quickly, in order to accommodate the growth. During a rough patch in the market in late 2007, the firm's performance began to deteriorate versus the Standard & Poor's 500—the primary benchmark against which they were judged by investors.

This was far from a unique scenario. If you follow the investment community, you know that every firm goes through periods of underperformance. The disturbing thing about *this* period, though, was that key employees began to quit the firm, for various stated and unstated reasons. As these people left, the firm's overall performance continued to deteriorate, and seemingly avoidable analytical mistakes became more and more common.

More concerned about the performance of his team than the firm's overall flagging economic performance, he called and asked whether I could come over to his office and speak with him. I listened for a few hours as he described his philosophy of the business. He spoke in a heartfelt way about the principles described above: teamwork, innovation, long-term thinking, and so on. It was inspirational—to such an extent that by the time he was finished, I was almost ready to sign up and work there myself. What a great place to learn and grow professionally!

Then the story took a less positive turn. He went on to describe the recent departures, the performance deterioration, and—worst of all, in his eyes—a series of avoidable mistakes in analyzing companies and stocks. As he spoke, I observed his irritation increasing—the volume and pitch of his voice rose until he was nearly shouting: "Why the hell is this *happening*?" He strode around his office, gesticulating as he yelled, "Why doesn't the team get it? Am I the only one who cares about our values? I feel like I'm alone, here. I've got the weight of the world on my shoulders. How did we get into this fix?"

I heard him out, not responding to his rhetorical questions (or his anger). Finally, I asked him whether I could meet with a handful of his key leaders one-on-one. He agreed to this, and I subsequently met with five of his senior leaders individually. In each of these sessions, I heard story after story about how the firm's leader conducted himself on a daily basis. It was eye-opening. For example:

- They told stories of the daily 8:30 a.m. investment staff meeting. In these meetings, the leader often directly criticized and browbeat individual staff members. If a stock went down, he was especially critical, wanting an explanation of why this had happened—even though everyone in the room knew that there might not actually be a cogent or clear answer to this question. (The stock market is not always driven by logic; sometimes, stocks simply go down for reasons that cannot be easily determined or explained.) If you were an investment staff member at this firm and you picked a stock that declined, you knew, for sure, that you were going to get "beat up" in front of your colleagues—even though the firm's leader had actively participated in, and agreed with, the decision to invest in that stock.

- I also heard about the unpredictable mood swings of the leader. "You never know from day to day," one person told me, "which person you're going to encounter: the happy one or the miserable one." It got worse. He was described as alternating between temper tantrums on one day and saccharine, over-the-top compliments the next. People walked on eggshells, not knowing what to expect. His mood might be driven by the fund's performance—or by something that happened at home before he came to work, or some other factor. Who could predict? How could you know?

- Another theme came through loud and clear: despite the firm's avowed emphasis on coaching, the leader really no longer had enough time to coach his staff of professionals. He was spread too thin, dealing with outside investors, administrative matters, investment decisions, asset allocation and portfolio construction, and so on. As one senior professional told me, "We've gotten so big, and he's out with investors so much more. To us, he's really become unapproachable, because he's so busy with other stuff."

What I was hearing was that the leader had failed fundamentally to delegate specific types of decisions to others (see chapter 4). As a result, essentially all administrative, investor relations, investment, and trading decisions had to be approved by him. This created an enormous bottleneck and undermined the leadership development as well as teamwork potential of the group. It also created a strange, almost surreal atmosphere when he publicly dressed down his colleagues for bad decisions: *doesn't he remember that he made that decision himself?*

Many of the senior leaders I interviewed were actively thinking about leaving because—as I heard many times, in so many words—"the fun has gone out of the job." I also heard a steady refrain that I found particularly troubling: "Please don't repeat these comments to him! Even if you don't tell him who made them, he'll *know*, and I'll be in the doghouse for the rest of my time with the firm."

Needless to say, I assured them I would do everything in my power to disguise all comments and conceal the identities of the individuals who made them. On that basis, they all gave me permission to relay their observations to the leader. Again, though, I was struck by the degree of reluctance and anxiety they were demonstrating as I obtained their permission to draw on their comments in my report to their boss. It wasn't just an awkward situation; it was a dysfunctional one.

I also was struck by how directly, and completely, these stories contradicted the goals and aspirations that the leader had articulated regarding the type of organization he wanted to build and sustain. Yes, he communicated them forcefully, and often. The problem, though, was that they no longer jibed with his daily behavior.

In my meetings with the managing partner, I first gave him the general flavor of what I had heard. Then I recommended that he hire an outside coach who would formally interview a very broad range of company employees—perhaps two dozen or more. (This, I figured, would prevent any one person from being identified and singled out for "punishment"; it would also make the findings harder to ignore, since they would be derived from a broader base.) I recommended a coach in whose work I had a lot of confidence, and recommended that she be brought on board as soon as possible. The leader agreed.

Two months passed, and I was called in to meet with the managing partner and discuss the results reported by the coach. He got right to the point. "How could they *say* those things?" he asked defensively.

By this time, he and I had a pretty good relationship, and I felt free to be blunt with him. I explained that the problem wasn't with the people who had been interviewed; the problem was with *him*. He was failing to acknowledge, or even realize, that his actions carried far more weight than his words. It didn't matter how many walls or Web sites he covered with those words; all too often, his behavior pointed in exactly the opposite direction.

We talked through the kinds of actions he took in a typical day, and why. Together, drawing on the coach's report and my earlier observations, we critiqued the worst of these actions and discussed the chilling impact they had on the people of the firm. More or less in real time, he saw that as a result of the gulf between what he espoused and what he actually did, he appeared to be a hypocrite.

This wasn't a comfortable conclusion to reach, and I give him credit for getting there. I give him even more credit for his efforts over the following months, as he slowly learned to change many of his more confusing and offensive behaviors.

It was a painful period for him. He needed to spend time trying to better understand his own motivations and behaviors—
including his assumptions about human nature—and come to
grips with why he behaved the way he did. A lot of it, he told
me at one point, had to do with his life story, his relationships
with his parents, the lessons (good and bad) that he had learned
from his early-career bosses, his overall temperament, and the
way he dealt with stress. Again, it was a tough, even searing,
process for him, but he learned to think before he acted, and to
weigh his actions as heavily as his words. He also learned that
he needed to delegate much more extensively, to make sure
that critical firm priorities were being pursued even when he
was too busy to address them himself.

In terms of concrete steps, he learned to develop several junior coaches who were willing and able to help him understand the impact of his behavior. With those coaches, and also
with friends and family members, he focused on enhancing his
self-awareness: seeing himself as others saw him. He also designated key lieutenants to whom he delegated various critical
tasks that were essential to achieving the vision of the firm.

Over the next few months, the company's atmosphere and
culture gradually improved, becoming more in line with the
leader's aspirations. Although the markets remained difficult,
the firm began performing dramatically better in comparison
with its competitors. In the surest sign that things were getting better—and the word was getting out—several former
employees who had jumped ship in the bad days agreed to return because of stories from their former colleagues about the
change in behavior of the CEO.

The Process of Self-Discovery

This case history is about self-discovery and understanding. It's about *you* understanding *you*. This is a critical challenge for a leader, and it's one to which we'll return in more depth in the next chapter. As your roles evolve from producer, to manager of a small team, to manager of a larger team, to having hundreds or thousands of employees, the pressures and the role-model requirements that you are expected to take on become dramatically more important.

Not every leader is conscious of this transition, and those who remain unaware of it are very likely to fail—without ever understanding exactly what went wrong. Success, in senior management positions, requires you to have an understanding of who you are, an appreciation of the power of the role you are in, a careful plan for delegating key responsibilities and empowering others, and a conscious approach to the messages you want to be sending with your behavior. Have you thought through these questions?

Learning to Lead Others

A very capable and seasoned senior executive was recruited to become the CEO of a diversified industrial company. He got the job when the company's board of directors did an external search after ousting their previous CEO. He went through an extensive interview process that was conducted in a highly discreet manner, given that this was a public company and the board wanted to keep rumors to a minimum.

Why did the board hire him? There were plenty of good reasons. Over the course of his career, he had proved to be a terrific production manager, and later an accomplished product manager, at three different companies. He had an impressive breadth of experience at those companies and was, at this point, in his early fifties. Given his relatively young age, he would have plenty of time to put his stamp on the company.

What the board *didn't* find out in its due diligence—in part due to the secrecy with which it was compelled to operate—were some of his weak points. For example, while he was an excellent strategist, he was not a particularly strong "people person." He didn't particularly enjoy developing deep relationships with his subordinates, through which he might learn about their strengths, weaknesses, backgrounds, and personalities. In addition, he was somewhat stingy about sharing credit, probably because of his own insecurities and his previous experiences. In fact, in his previous jobs, he had concluded that in order to get ahead, he needed to make sure that he got the credit for key accomplishments. Last, although he was a great producer himself, he had trouble developing relationships with other top producers and was not particularly adept at coaching others to become great producers.

The board learned, to its dismay, that many of the strengths that had propelled its new CEO up the ladder at his previous employers were not necessarily the qualities that would make him a success as CEO of this company. Upon observing him for several months and hearing feedback from several company employees, the board had an intervention with the CEO.

Having done their homework, the board members presented him with a series of issues they believed he needed to address if he was to succeed as CEO.

At this point, the lead director asked me to help in this situation. While the CEO was deficient in a number of areas, he was nevertheless a very talented person. He was quite shaken by the board confrontation and was highly motivated to improve and make this situation successful.

We spoke at length through the various questions outlined in this book, including the importance of the CEO's being a role model. To respond to the board's constructive concerns, he decided to develop an informal network of junior coaches at the company, with whom he could consult one-on-one regarding the impact of his behavior. He also decided that despite his previous training and development of potentially bad habits, he absolutely could learn to change, become a role model, and build a cohesive company. I was extremely impressed by the fact that once he committed himself to thinking differently about his role as CEO and committing himself to learning, he made substantial progress.

I am pleased to report that after a year of intensive work and discussion, he is performing at a very high level. He always had the intelligence, technical capabilities, and other talents that he needed—in fact, he had those qualities in abundance. The challenge, for him, lay in *changing the way he thought about his role*. The CEO job, he learned, is about a lot more than performing tasks. It is about being open to learning and changing, setting an example for others, and communicating through actions as well as words.

Can you still learn and improve, as a senior manager in your early fifties? The answer is absolutely yes—if you are committed and motivated. In addition, as a younger professional, you should be highly motivated to work on developing skills and practices that will prepare you for more senior positions as your career progresses.

From the 180-Pound Executive to the 800-Pound Gorilla

The CEO of a large consulting firm wanted advice regarding certain pressing strategy and leadership issues. He had spent thirty years at this company before recently being promoted to CEO. I had known him during my own career in investment banking, and had advised him at various points during his upward career climb. I liked him very much. He was always very bright and insightful. He had a very dry, sometimes off-color sense of humor. He had always been a bit of a cynic, but that was a humorous and generally appealing part of his personality.

This company was very large and—given its size and place in its industry—very high profile. The CEO called me one day and got right to the point. He was off to a "rough start" at the company, he said. First, he had done an in-person meeting with institutional investors and sell-side analysts, and he didn't think it had gone very well. In addition, he wasn't sure he had been approaching his direct reports and company employees in the right way. I told him honestly that I wasn't sure exactly what he was talking about. After a brief pause, he asked whether, as a favor, I would meet with two or three of his direct reports and ask how they thought he was doing.

I agreed to do this, and within the week, had the conversations that he had requested. What I learned was that these direct reports had been thrilled that he had been named CEO. Having said this, they had expected him to recognize that he needed to behave differently now that he was CEO. The cynicism they used to enjoy now seemed inappropriate, and they wished he would stop it. For example, they didn't want him using the company's town hall meetings as an opportunity to make cynical comments. They wanted their own subordinates to be idealistic about the company, and that required the CEO to show he was a "true believer." Even if it was only a role, they told me, they expected him to play it!

There was more—mostly variations on the theme of his new role. They wanted him to drop the off-color jokes, even in private settings. They thought that he needed to get in earlier in the morning. True, he had always been a late arriver—it had been the subject of much friendly banter, over the years—but they believed that because he was now the CEO, his tardiness was sending a bad signal to employees. They also wanted him to talk with his assistant about being a bit friendlier and more constructive when she received calls regarding his schedule. They suggested that he should think about driving a less flashy car to work and be a bit more mindful of his dress, even on casual Fridays. In short, they wanted him to look and act like the CEO of a conservative company.

When I sat down with my friend and relayed all of this news to him, he was both amused and perturbed. He explained that, for the past thirty years, he had never gotten any such feedback; now all of a sudden, everybody had an opinion about the way he *dressed*? He confessed that he thought that many of the comments were off base, even ridiculous—and besides, was he supposed to change his act at this stage in his life?

We had been friends for several years, so I felt free to talk to him in a fairly blunt way. He had to realize, I said, that he had made a major transition: from a 180-pound senior executive to the 800-pound gorilla that embodied the hopes, dreams, and aspirations of thousands of people. Like it or not, his *every move* would now be closely observed, for the rest of his career. His statements would be parsed internally and externally. His moods would be observed, tracked, interpreted. How he behaved in restaurants, how he talked to the custodial staff, how he dealt with employees across the company— all would be closely scrutinized henceforth for clues to his character.

In short, he had become "role model in chief," and—I told him—this was part and parcel of accepting the job as CEO. Sure, he might *feel* the same as he did four months earlier, but to everyone around him, he was *not* the same. His words and actions all had more weight. Yes, he needed to be himself, but he also needed to recalibrate his behavior, taking into account his new weight and strength. A kind word from him now meant more to an employee than it ever had before; a rebuke from him stung far worse than in his previous life.

The good news is that, over a period of time, he took all of this feedback on board and eventually became quite comfortable with his new reality. But it definitely required a change in his mind-set. His world would be different, from now on.

Promotions: A Powerful Signal About Who You Are and What You Value

The role-model analysis is not just about your behavior. It also relates to the behavior of those you promote. Just as you are a powerful role model, the people you promote to key jobs send enormously powerful signals to the organization about what *you* truly believe. Are these decisions consistent with your values and your vision for the organization? Do these leaders share your vision and buy into your carefully chosen priorities for the organization? Are these leaders the type of role models you want your employees to emulate?

The CEO of a professional services firm was in the midst of attempting a strategic repositioning of his company. His objective was to expand the services his company provided and move into new advisory businesses that were adjacent to the company's traditional business. I thought the strategy made a lot of sense and was consistent with the firm's distinctive competencies, and that there was a terrific market opportunity to provide these additional services to the firm's clients.

From my firsthand observations, I believed that this leader was an excellent role model. He not only articulated the central values and vision for the firm, but also was very scrupulous about *leading from the front*—that is, making sure that his behavior was consistent and exemplified the qualities that he wanted his leaders to exhibit in this firm: commitment to excellence, putting the client's interests first, coaching and mentoring top talent, and establishing an atmosphere of fairness.

Despite these built-in advantages, he was struggling to figure out how to execute the strategic repositioning that he had
been advocating. He had personally chosen his senior lieutenants since he had become CEO two years earlier. He himself
had always been a superb producer before becoming the firm's
leader, and he naturally gravitated toward promoting other
producers—that is, people like him—into key senior roles. In
other words, when he made promotion decisions, he was willing to overlook shortcomings in his people's leadership skills,
coaching skills, and moral compasses because he valued revenue generation far above these other attributes. Initially, this
seemed to work; but over time, voluntary turnover among the
top-performing quartile of professionals began to increase,
and it became more difficult to move professionals between
divisions.

I suggested that he ask his head of HR to interview a number
of midlevel managers to learn more about the increased turnover. I also suggested that the HR head do exit interviews—
even if they had to be held a few months after the employee
left the firm—to find out the reasons behind the departures.
Finally, I suggested that he add some interviews with midlevel
managers who *hadn't* left the company—yet. I agreed to meet
with the head of HR first, to debrief what he learned, and then
join him for a meeting with the CEO.

The HR head had an instinct, before doing the interviews,
about what he might find. The interviews confirmed his expectations. He heard that while the CEO espoused values of
fairness and valuing the employee, the division heads he had
put in place sent very different signals, indeed. No amount
of speeches from the CEO or exemplary behavior on his part

could make up for the behavior of his key subordinates. The constant refrain encountered by the HR head was that *production is the be-all and end-all at this company*. If that *wasn't* the case, why did the CEO fail to choose subordinates who exhibited the behaviors he was touting? Why did he always go for the producers?

The midlevel employees who had remained with the company were quite cynical about the new strategic initiatives and didn't want to sign up for them. While these new directions might make strategic sense for the company, they involved a substantial degree of risk. In particular, years would have to pass before production in the new businesses reached the same level as in the existing businesses. And if production was the critical metric—as evidenced by all those promotion decisions—why should someone who was succeeding at an existing position decide to move, and thereby incur a risk? It also emerged that the division heads were actively discouraging key subordinates from moving into these new areas, because losing them might detract from production in their own divisions.

Next, we discussed all this with the CEO, who was quite disturbed by this feedback. I encouraged him to first actively coach his key subordinates on what he expected of them. He should explicitly expand the criteria for compensation to include factors other than pure production. He should assure people who were transferring to the new areas that he would personally watch over their compensation and career progress.

He agreed to this approach. Unfortunately, though, he realized after only a few months that over the previous several years, he had promoted the wrong people into certain key jobs. He was now learning firsthand what many in the company had known all along: that his promotion decisions had been contradicting what he had been articulating as the vision and key priorities for the firm. With each promotion, he was creating a negative role model, which eventually undermined his ability to build his organization and move it forward. Yes, he ultimately was able to correct many of these mistakes—but valuable time was lost, and the progress that the firm made (and *had* to make) was delayed unnecessarily.

What do these stories add up to? They add up to the fact that both you *and* the people you select as your lieutenants are *role models* and are therefore carefully observed by your people. This is why many companies have training sessions for professionals who have been recently promoted to more senior positions. In these sessions, they help the participants better understand the new skills and practices they will need to learn, as well as their increased visibility as role models in the organization.

How Do You Behave Under Pressure?

Many executives deeply understand their position as role model and manage their behavior accordingly. In many cases, this works well until there is a crisis in which the executive comes under enormous pressure. This circumstance is worth exploring here in more depth. While a leader is closely observed under normal circumstances, in a crisis, you can multiply that scrutiny by a factor of ten. You may not be aware of it, but when a highly adverse or extremely stressful situation develops, your people begin to watch every move you make with the intensity of a hawk. They want to see who you really are and what you truly value.

While crises might represent only a fraction of your time as a leader, these episodes are the ones that are likely to *define you*. This isn't necessarily fair, or rational, but anecdotes about you under pressure are normally the ones that live on and make the rounds in your company. When your people go out for drinks after work, your behavior under pressure is very likely what they're going to talk about.

People take their cues from the way you behave when things are not going well. Do you lose your temper? Do you become moody? Do you distance yourself from the situation? Do you blame others—to the point that they question whether you really believe in teamwork? Should they avoid bringing you bad news because you have a tendency to shoot the messenger? Should they be wary of approaching you if they think you're in a bad mood? By your behavior, do you train them to worry more about themselves, versus the company, because that's what *you* do, in a pinch?

Learning to manage your behavior in times of stress is a critical attribute of a leader. You need to learn this skill.

What Creates "Pressure" for You?

Think about what creates pressure for *you*. My emphasis on *you* is purposeful. Pressure and stress are deeply person-specific. The issues that stress you out may not bother someone else at all, and vice versa.

For example: some of my hot buttons include people quitting unexpectedly, lax attitudes, and finger-pointing. On the other hand, I am not particularly bothered if we lose a piece of business (as long as I believe we have put forth our best effort). It doesn't bother me to admit a mistake; in fact, I find it liberating to get something off my chest and out in the open. Similarly, I don't mind taking responsibility for things that don't go well. I believe that's the first step toward diagnosing the problem, fixing the mistake, and moving forward. In stressful situations, I have learned (and am still learning) to count to ten, not overreact, and stay calm when I feel anxious.

What's on your list of stressors? It might include, for example, not getting promoted, losing money, getting fired, firing someone, confrontation, believing you're not smart enough, believing you're not liked or loved, feeling overloaded, and so on and so forth.

Striving for Greater Self-Awareness as You Become a Leader

As you think about what circumstances create undue pressure for you, and, further, consider your typical behavior in response to these stresses, you should develop potential action steps that will help you cope with pressure. Action steps could be as simple as cutting down on your caffeine consumption, getting a proper night's rest, regular exercise, or meditation. Other actions could include giving yourself a brief time-out before you overreact to a stressful situation, building more slack time into your weekly schedule, or developing a stronger support group comprising confidantes both inside and outside your firm.

This advice may seem a bit touchy-feely to you, but I can tell you that self-awareness and self-management are critically important attributes as you move up in your career. These aspects of your behavior become especially important when you become a leader, because your behavior will be observed and imitated by your people. If you have bad habits under stress, you should expect that your people will adopt those same bad habits. This can severely undermine the trust and confidence in your leadership and, as a consequence, undermine the operating effectiveness of your organization.

Of course, you are not going to be able to avoid stressful situations. Stress is a part of being human, and it's certainly part of leadership. You can't run away from stress. Instead, you need to become much more deliberate about how you choose to *respond* to stress.

The Cost of Playing the Blame Game

As I mentioned earlier, some people can't stand to admit that they were wrong, or that they've made a mistake. You could put a loaded gun to their heads, and they *still* would not want to admit that they screwed up. Unfortunately, these people have not yet learned that making the mistake is rarely fatal. On the other hand, failing to own up to it and address the issue can have severe negative consequences for a leader. It becomes a severe issue when the leader fails to take ownership of a problem, distances him or herself from it, or points the finger at others. This reaction to stress has a chilling impact on teamwork. It discourages subordinates from pulling together and working collaboratively to improve the situation.

I recently advised a leader who was very careful to avoid responsibility for difficult problems that arose during the "Great Recession." These problems were not at all unusual in his industry. This difficult period, though, brought out many of the insecurities and fears that this leader had been feeling during his career. His response was to distribute the blame in numerous different directions in order to deflect attention from him. He blamed his predecessor, his subordinates, certain of his suppliers, and even his customers. He cast himself as a victim who had inherited a "bad hand."

What happened next? His predecessor—offended by remarks attributed to him in the newspaper—decided to strike back in an equally public way to defend his reputation. Because he was still a revered, even legendary figure among the company's employees, people inside and outside the company took note.

All this had a chilling impact across the company. The consensus among the employees was that the current CEO—who had been in charge for more than a year and had the ultimate responsibility—should have simply taken ownership, looked forward, and mobilized employees to develop action plans for what to do next. By blaming others, he severely damaged his own reputation, undermined the confidence of existing employees, and hurt the company's "franchise." People who would have been inclined to help him address the company's challenges decided it was better to keep a distance from this CEO. They learned that helping him could lead to being blamed if the help did not work out positively. Morale at the company is still repairing itself, very slowly, in the wake of this episode.

Helping Your People Cope with Stress

As a leader, you are accountable for both your own behavior and that of your employees. As a result, it is wise to discuss the issue of behavior under pressure with your people.

As noted earlier, the recent economic crisis and its aftermath put enormous pressure on people in a wide range of industries and companies. In the extreme, it sometimes revealed severe vulnerabilities in organizations whose primary driver during the crisis was "making money," versus maintaining and building the franchise. The crisis presented numerous opportunities to help clients—or, alternatively, to take short-term financial advantage of them because of extreme economic conditions. In retrospect, the superb companies were those led by executives who emphasized the importance of using the crisis to enhance their relationships with key clients and thereby build their sustainable long-term business franchises.

As we discussed in chapter 1, a clear vision with priorities is vital to a successful company. In the midst of an economic crisis, this vision can serve as an anchor and a beacon that guide leadership and employee behavior. On the other hand, if your corporate ethic is to *make money at all costs*, you are likely to be putting people under the kind of pressure that is very likely to lead to franchise damage at best and potential ethical lapses at worst.

This is why it is critical, during a crisis, to overcommunicate the vision and key priorities for your firm. In this context, it is also critical to think about the business you're in, and anticipate the types of lapses that are likely to occur when your people are put under pressure. This pressure could emanate from fear of losing money, fear of losing their jobs, fear of letting down their peers, and so on. In the end, though, the pressure they are feeling is likely to be primarily coming from *you*.

There's a speech that I've given, in one version or another, during every economic downturn in which I have managed a group of people. I tell my people *not* to cut corners, and not to give in to pressure to generate revenue in ways that are contrary to serving clients and are inconsistent with our values. If they are in doubt, I encourage them to elevate their questions (to more senior leaders of the company) until they feel confident about what actions they should take. I tell them that they should err on the side of doing what's right for the client and *building the franchise*. Take good care of our clients, *especially* in the bad times. We're going to get through this period, and we're going to be around for a long time. Let's build this business.

In times of stress, overcommunicate with your people, and especially your senior lieutenants. Your senior reports are role models, and they are being scrutinized by their subordinates. In addition, they are human. Maybe they are afraid for their jobs. Maybe they're overleveraged at home and need money. Maybe they're ambitious and angling for that next promotion. I try to spend substantial amounts of time with my senior people during these difficult periods, and talk candidly about stress and how they are dealing with it.

If handled properly, this approach can dramatically improve the role-modeling behavior of your people—and help ensure that you and your organization emerge from crises better positioned to compete.

Becoming a Role Model

In this chapter, we've emphasized the leader's role as a model for the behavior of others. Words and deeds both matter, and must be consistent. We've also explored the special circumstance of severe pressure, and how the leader must be self-aware enough to understand what creates severe stress for her, and then carefully monitor her behavior during these periods to ensure that it is consistent with the values and principles she is trying to establish in her organization.

We've discussed several ideas about how you can better manage stress for yourself and your people. In my own life and career, I have found that saving my money, avoiding living beyond my means, keeping a regular journal, and maintaining some type of emotional balance through nonprofit work and other interests have all helped to keep me sane during difficult periods. I have shared these approaches with my students and encouraged them to develop a few of their own.

I have also found it very useful to be emotionally prepared to "walk away." This means realizing that you can live without *this* job. To do this, it helps to believe that your whole life is not wrapped into others' assessment of your job performance. It also helps to have developed a vision and set of ethical principles that you steadfastly refuse to violate, even under severe pressure. Of course, these stress relievers can take time to develop—both time in your career and years in your life as you develop greater emotional maturity.

It pays to think about these issues today. Exploring ways to create some emotional detachment and independence should enhance your ability to be a better role model, perform at a higher level, and distinguish yourself in periods of stress.

Suggested Follow-up Steps

1. Write down two or three key messages you believe you send with your behavior (versus your speeches). Seek advice from key subordinates and advisers who directly observe your behavior, in order to answer this question: is there a "disconnect" between the messages you wish to send and those you are in fact sending?

2. Do this same exercise for your key direct reports. What messages is each of them sending about what is truly valued in your organization? Again, make discreet inquiries, if necessary, to do this analysis. Incorporate this work into your coaching of these executives.

3. Think of a situation in which you felt enormous stress at work and regretted your behavior. Write down the one or two issues that created the stress you were feeling— acknowledging that these issues may have had nothing to do with work. How would you behave differently if you could replay this situation? Write down one or two lessons you take away from this exercise.

7

Reaching Your Potential

Being True to Yourself

> Are you pursuing a path that is consistent with your
> assessment of your strengths, weaknesses, and passions?
>
> If not, what are you waiting for?
>
> Have you developed your own style at work?
>
> Do you speak up, express your opinions, and conduct
> yourself with confidence?
>
> Do you encourage your people to be authentic and
> express their opinions?

The previous chapters of this book focused on questions leaders should ask in order to more effectively run their organizations. Many of these questions require you to break old habits, learn new ones, and ask new questions. Essentially, much of the material in the previous chapters involved "blocking and tackling"—in other words, practical suggestions for how you might develop your leadership skills and more effectively run your organization. Very likely you will take on board those ideas and suggestions that resonate with you and have relevance to your organizational context.

Now we'll move on to a subject that typically separates good leaders from great ones. This subject is deeply personal. The focus of this chapter is *you*.

In this chapter, we will focus on your philosophical approach to your work. I will challenge you to develop a deeper understanding of your talents, personality, values, and passions. This discussion will be based on the premise that in order to be an outstanding leader, you must understand yourself and consciously bring your unique qualities and personality to work every day. I strongly believe that excellent organizations are run by leaders who bring their distinctive attributes to the job and encourage their people to do the same. In doing this, they get the most out of themselves and their organizations.

Superb leaders are constantly learning and adapting. They are learning about the world, their industry, and the people around them—but in particular, they are learning about themselves. This learning evolves at every stage of their life and career.

In this chapter, we will explore the importance of understanding your own strengths and weaknesses, as well as your passions. I will emphasize the importance of learning from others—but at the same time, developing a leadership style that fits *you*.

We also will consider whether you are being too careful in expressing your opinions at work, and how this can ultimately hold you back. This chapter also will raise the question of whether you are confident enough to be yourself at work, or whether you are trying to be someone who you think you're *supposed* to be—perhaps someone who you imagine that your boss, your family, or your friends want you to be?

In addition to these questions, we will address the importance of creating an atmosphere at work where your people are encouraged to be authentic and reach their unique potential. Great companies tend to be led by leaders who are comfortable being themselves, and who create an environment where their people can be themselves, too. In this way, both individuals and their organizations are able to reach their full potential.

Understanding Your Strengths and Weaknesses

Do you understand your strengths and weaknesses? Could you write them down on a piece of paper? Would your colleagues agree with these lists? If you're a junior professional, have you developed colleagues and senior coaches to help you with this? Looking back to chapter 3, if you're a senior leader, do you have junior coaches who can help you answer these questions? Do you take steps to work on your weaknesses, and take advantage of your unique strengths?[1]

A recently appointed CEO had previously spent his career taking on a succession of increasingly senior roles at four different companies. In recent years, he had been the CFO and then the head of a large division at a diversified industrial products company. Highly regarded in industry circles, he was recruited to be the CEO of a global industrial products company located in the upper Midwest. His new employer felt fortunate to have landed him as its new CEO.

After eight months on the job, he felt that he was struggling in his efforts to get off to a good start. He called me to ask whether I'd be willing to sit down with him to discuss his leadership style and perhaps give him some tips about how he could be more effective.

When we met, I first asked him to describe his three biggest strengths and his three biggest weaknesses. In his response, he gave me a pretty thorough and candid summary on both sides of the ledger. I learned that in his previous job as a division head, the CEO had given him a very thorough and rigorous review. Unfortunately, many of the strengths he listed were not particularly relevant to his current position, and most of the weaknesses bore directly on his current position as CEO. We discussed the fact that the division head role is actually quite different from the role of CEO. For example, in his new job as CEO, he had to communicate much more—externally, on television, and to a range of new constituents. Also, to be successful in the new job, he had to be much better at picking strong leaders for division head roles—as well as picking critical staff jobs (such as an HR head, a CFO, and a head of IT)—than he had been previously. In the past, he had often been more focused on *competing* with these types of people than on assessing them and selecting them to be part of his team.

We discussed the core tasks at which he would need to excel to be superb in his current job. I asked him to think carefully about identifying those specific tasks and consider the types of skills that he would need to develop—either himself or through building his team—in order to carry them out.

These were not questions that he could answer on the spot. He spent the next several weeks studying the characteristics of the CEOs at key competitors. He already knew some of them, and in the case of those he didn't know personally, he found enough public resources to give him insight into their approaches to their jobs. At the same time, he sought counsel from several of his direct reports regarding *their* opinions of his strengths and weaknesses relative to the demands of his current position. His direct reports responded very positively to these questions. No previous senior corporate leader had ever asked them for this kind of input before, and they were flattered and eager to help.

We then had a follow-up discussion. On the basis of his updated assessment of his strengths and weaknesses, and with only a little coaching from me, he came up with a developmental plan to help him improve in a few key areas. For example, he realized that he needed help with public speaking, and therefore hired a speech coach. Media relations was a critical area for improvement, and in response to his request, his in-house communications group put together a "seminar for one" on media training, investor relations, and how to speak with reporters.

Equally important, he thought more about his strengths and how to draw on them more fully. By all accounts, including his own, he was far more analytical than either of his two predecessors. He knew that his board had hired him in part because it wanted to inject more rigorous analysis into the company's decision making, and he was well equipped to accomplish that goal. He concluded that as long as he didn't overdo it, this could be an important distinctive competency that he could bring to his new job.

When we finished, the CEO decided that this was a very valuable exercise for him—so much so, that he decided to do it on a regular basis. He would keep a running checklist of personal strengths and weaknesses, which he would regularly update with the help of feedback from others. In that spirit, he resolved to build a cadre of junior coaches, who would help him maintain an accurate self-assessment and ensure that he kept a finger on the corporate pulse. He would regularly get their critique after a public speaking engagement or a television appearance.

Months later, he reported that he believed he had dramatically improved his strengths and addressed key weaknesses. Just as important, he had developed new coaching and "early warning" relationships throughout the company, all of which also raised his stature in the eyes of his key subordinates and employees. It was a success story that would have seemed unlikely only a few months earlier.

A Lifelong Process: When You're Through Learning, You're Through

Learning about your strengths and weaknesses is a never-ending process. It needs to be updated for each successive job you take. It doesn't end when you become CEO (or whatever leadership post you aspire to). Even if you never change jobs again, *your job will continue to change*. The world changes, and the needs of the business change. As a result, your strengths and weaknesses, relative to the needs of the job, also change. Like it or not, you have to be open to updating your views in this area and be willing to learn and improve. Very often, reaching your desired leadership position—and making a success of the opportunity—will challenge you to keep learning about yourself and building on your skills.

By the way: this exercise is *not* just for emerging or more senior executives. In fact, it should be adopted as early as possible in your career. It is also a mind-set that, for the reasons described above, needs to have some *permanence in your repertoire*. Don't make the mistake of discarding it later in your career, when—by all appearances—you're a "big success."

When you're through learning, you're through. How often have you heard some version of this saying? Do you take it to heart? Are you committed to learning for the rest of your life? I urge you to make this commitment; it is an indispensable quality of being an outstanding leader.

Recognizing Your Passions

As a leader, you do need to be aware of what you enjoy. In particular, which tasks do you really enjoy and which would you prefer not to do yourself?

What you delegate, how you structure your job, whether or not you are in the right job—all of this should flow from and be influenced by a realistic understanding of your likes and dislikes. If you hate doing something, you are likely to avoid it. Conversely, if you love doing something, you are likely to arrange your time so you can do more and more of it.

The question then becomes, how do your passions coincide with the needs of the business? Have you reconciled your passions with these business needs?

The CEO of a nursing home/health services company in Europe was very discouraged about her struggles to manage a number of her key employees. She became so discouraged, in fact, that she was questioning whether she wanted to continue to be CEO of the firm. She asked to come see me to discuss this. During our meeting, she vented about the various frustrations she was experiencing—including unusually high turnover among her senior facilities-management staff, as well as various back-office struggles, computer system failures, and so on.

I surprised her a bit by asking her first what she *loved* about the business: "Why in the world did you choose to take this job?" She thought for a few seconds, and then said that she truly loved helping people in need—the firm's clientele. She was enormously motivated by developing (and then executing) senior housing concepts that improved the quality of life for senior citizens and those with chronic health conditions. She was extremely good at understanding the customers' needs and then devising solutions to fit those needs. She got a thrill out of it!

Then I asked her what he *hated* about her job. She hesitated, but finally confessed that she really didn't enjoy the day-to-day management of the facilities, recruiting talent, or coaching young people. I asked how that could be possible, given that she had built a firm of more than a thousand people and had achieved a record of consistent success.

She explained that in the early years, she was so excited to be building a business of her own that she took the time to recruit and coach. Once the company developed a track record, however, she reverted to doing the things she loved best. In some ways, this made sense—after all, she was a superb conceptual thinker and also loved spending time with the company's clients. In other ways, though, it was a disaster in the making. The company's key facilities management, coaching, people development, and recruiting functions were allowed to atrophy. As the organization grew in size, this neglect became a bigger and bigger problem.

We discussed the fact that leaving these key tasks poorly attended to—even unattended—didn't make much sense. On the other hand, not everything had to be done by her, personally (see chapter 4). She needed to identify (or hire) a senior leader who would be empowered to lead the recruiting effort, take responsibility for coaching key staff, and identify other leaders who would extend the coaching effort still further.

After our discussions, she asked one of her senior leaders to fill the newly created position of chief operating officer (COO). In this role, the new COO was directly responsible for addressing these key facilities operation and talent development/coaching needs. He was someone who knew the company and its culture and thoroughly enjoyed the critical tasks the job called for. He was very effective, and this created more room for the CEO to focus on the essential tasks at which she was superb.

Our work was not quite over. In subsequent discussions, I stressed the fact that the CEO could not simply "punt" altogether on the coaching and people development front. I suggested that she needed to think of those elements of coaching that she *did* enjoy and could do effectively. After thinking about it, she realized that she did love to sit down with junior executives, discuss new development projects, and brainstorm about ideas for better serving clients. She agreed that she could, and should, do this more frequently.

Six months after the conclusion of these discussions, I received an update from her. She told me that she was far hap-

pier and that the company was operating much more effectively. She admitted that she was a bit amazed that the "fixes"
were so easy.

Passion for What You Do: Achieving Sustained High Performance

Perhaps this story seems simple, and its lessons obvious. How
could this leader have failed to see that she was neglecting tasks
so fundamental to the business? How could she not recognize
that she should delegate these tasks if she couldn't stand to do
them herself? In my experience, this circumstance is not as unusual as you might think. Many executives believe that there
are certain key tasks they must do themselves, whether or not
they fit their competencies or interests. They believe it is a sign
of weakness to delegate these tasks. As a result of this view,
they perform those tasks poorly or irregularly.

Ask yourself, do you neglect important tasks you don't enjoy,
and fail to delegate them to others? Do you focus most of your
time on the tasks you really do enjoy, at the same time leaving other important functions unattended? Ask yourself these
questions, face up to the answers, and then—if necessary—
develop an action plan to proactively deal with the situation.

Again, as emphasized in previous chapters, you have to
match your time to the organization's key priorities. Having
said this, you also have to *enjoy* those selected tasks if you're
going to do them on a sustainable basis—that is, at a high level
of excellence. Consider whether you do have sufficient passion
for those tasks you choose to spend time on.

This is a critical area of advice that I regularly give to MBA students as they are thinking about their first job and industry choice. The prospect of financial gain is a strong motivator for many young people. Unfortunately, financial rewards typically take years to achieve, and they typically come only through sustained outstanding performance. It's tough to perform at an outstanding level for a sustained period if you don't enjoy what you're doing! This is a critical lesson for young professionals who are just starting their careers and want to get started on a path to success.

Once you become a more senior professional, the nature of your job is likely to change. Among other things, you gain the opportunity to delegate key tasks. Invariably, as a more senior leader, you will enjoy certain tasks more than others. For those tasks for which you lack passion, consider delegating primary responsibility to someone who *will* have the passion. I recommend you take this one step further and make sure that your direct reports undertake this same exercise.

No, I am not suggesting that all key tasks have to be enjoyable. Certain tasks that come with the territory of being a leader—for example, deciding compensation and promotions, conducting reviews, and firing people—range from being a pain in the neck to being downright unpleasant. A leader has to learn to spend time on and embrace these activities. I am suggesting that, when possible, executives should concentrate their time on tasks that fit their skills and their passions—and make sure that, whether they do tasks themselves or delegate them, these critical responsibilities are getting accomplished at a high level of quality that fits the needs of the organization.

Developing an Effective Leadership Style That Fits Who You Are

There's another aspect to "being yourself," beyond recognizing and accommodating your passions. To be effective, you need to develop a leadership style that fits who you are.

Your "leadership style" is the manner in which you do your job. There are a number of questions you could ask yourself to tease out the fundamental elements of your style. For example: Do you like to joke around, or are you by nature a more serious person? Would you prefer to meet with people one-on-one or in groups? Do you prefer being blunt and direct, or would you rather be less confrontational? Are you highly analytical (learn by doing extensive analyses), or do you learn more by talking to people, or do you like a combination of the two? What is your theory of human motivation—do you believe people need a club over their heads to perform, or do you believe that, given clear direction and coaching, people are highly motivated to excel, and you simply need to give them the proper incentives?

The answers to these kinds of questions have a powerful influence on how you behave every day and how you approach your job. Each person is likely to answer these questions in a manner that feels right to him or her and fits his or her distinctive emotional needs. Fortunately, there is not just one effective leadership style. There are many, and in any given situation, one or more could be highly effective.

The challenge for you is to develop a leadership style that fits not only who you are but also the needs of your enterprise (the situation). If your style doesn't fit who you are, it is unlikely to be sustainable. On the other hand, if your leadership style fits you but doesn't fit the demands of the situation, you are unlikely to be successful. Of course, this challenge is intensified when the situation changes due to external forces or other factors. One of the ongoing challenges of being an effective leader, over a sustained period of time, is to make the course corrections to your leadership style that are necessary to keep the organization on track and yet fit your personality and distinctive traits.[1]

Leadership style is a concept worth thinking about in your very first job. It will invariably involve a bit of trial and error as you try different approaches and take on new job assignments. My primary advice to young professionals is to begin this process as soon as possible—don't wait until you become a more senior professional!

It Helps to Write It Down

Have you thought sufficiently about this? Could you write down the fundamentals of your leadership style? I encourage you to try it—right now. Pick up a notepad or your iPad, and write a few sentences that describe your leadership style.

Any surprises? The process of writing down your style causes you to think about how you go about doing things, and recognize your underlying assumptions. Many people don't consciously think about whether they prefer one-on-one or group meetings, or how they actually go about doing their jobs. When they actually reflect on it, they may not be altogether pleased with their modus operandi—and they may realize that it isn't as effective as they'd like.

Do you feel good about your style? Is it effective? Does it fit your values? Were you wincing as you wrote down its component parts? What made you wince, and why?

Are You Willing to Hear the Truth, Learn, and Adapt Your Behavior?

A senior executive of a large industrial firm was informed by his CEO that there was a serious undercurrent of dissatisfaction in the ranks of the division he was leading. This senior executive was surprised, and disagreed with the CEO about that assessment. To help resolve this dispute, he and the CEO agreed that the executive should take additional steps to get a reality check. The CEO urged him to have a conversation with me and see what happened from there.

At the beginning of our first discussion, the executive made it quite clear that he was in strong disagreement with the CEO's assessment, which had been based on a 360-degree review of him (along with the rest of the top fifty executives in the company). He believed the process was flawed and amounted to more of a popularity contest than an objective assessment of his skills and effectiveness.

Early on in this discussion, I asked him whether he could describe his leadership style. He responded with a string of platitudes right out of the pop leadership literature. "I believe in getting the right people in the right seats," he began. "I believe in giving people the tools they need and enough running room to prove themselves. I believe that you have to create an environment in which people can excel. I believe in being tough but fair. I believe in an open-door policy." And so on, and so on. I didn't argue, but I *did* point out that the 360-degree review suggested his style was quite different from the one he was describing. I suggested that rather than relying solely on the 360-degree review, I would be willing to do brief interviews with a small subset of his top executives. He enthusiastically agreed to this.

We met again in four weeks. I gave him a candid assessment of what I heard in my meetings:

> *He doesn't listen. He doesn't ask questions—he just advocates. When I meet with him, he does all the talking. He doesn't coach me; in fact, he hasn't taken the time to get to know me at all. He likes to recite slogans about what I should be doing, but he doesn't have any specific actionable advice because he really doesn't understand me, my job, or my business unit. He doesn't like to hear about problems. He tends to avoid me when I do have a problem, or blame me for having the problem. He tells different things to different people about the same situation. He is intimidating: he makes it clear that my loyalty should be to him, and if he ever heard me complaining publicly about an issue, he would take it as a personal betrayal. He doesn't like open debate on issues. He makes decisions unilaterally, but then pretends that we were part of the decision because "we discussed it."*

He was quite shaken to hear all this. Why hadn't he heard this feedback before from these people? He realized that it was partly because he had never asked these people for direct feedback—and, in addition, he gave off a vibe that he didn't want feedback. He was starting to realize that his actual leadership style was quite different from the canned slogans he espoused.

The questions now were: how could he not recognize that these issues existed among his subordinates? Did he want to address these issues, and was he willing to develop a leadership style that was more effective in this situation? If so, how should he go about doing this?

First, I gave him an assignment. "Write down a *real* description of your style," I told him. "Not the polished sales pitch you gave me last time. If you need to, go out and interview a subset of your senior lieutenants and ask for their help. Pick the ones you're closest to, if that's the easiest way for you to get started. Tell them you want to dig a bit deeper to get specific feedback regarding your style and how you are perceived.

"When you believe you have an accurate depiction that you're willing to discuss," I continued, "call me. If you feel this is a waste of time, then let's drop the whole exercise. No pressure, honestly—you won't offend me if you don't call me back at all. Keep in mind that you're doing this for *you*, not for me."

I heard from him three weeks later. He had taken this exercise very seriously, and written out an honest appraisal of his style based on conversations with a number of his subordinates and some real soul-searching. As we spoke, he explained that his style had been developed over many years. It had grown out of his observations of previous bosses, from whom he had borrowed and adapted various tools and techniques. He believed— for example—that a leader needed to know the answers, be a strong advocate for his or her point of view, demonstrate confidence, and avoid showing any uncertainties or vulnerabilities.

By interviewing his subordinates and thinking about what he had heard, and by talking with me, he now realized that he had a golden opportunity as a rising division leader to develop a leadership style that fit his personality and did not depend on him being Superman. Maybe—just maybe—he could be more effective, and stronger, if he asked more questions, listened harder, tried to understand what his people were thinking, and admitted to not having all the answers. Maybe this change in style would enhance, rather than detract from, his chances of eventually being CEO, either at this company or at another firm.

Up to this point, he thought that the role of the leader was to shoulder by himself the burdens of the entire company. Given the complex nature of his business, this was an enormously difficult assignment, and on a fundamental level, it really wasn't effective. Now he saw a different way forward, based on a new leadership style.

What do *you* truly believe? What feels comfortable for you? Is your style based on your own conception of what a great leader does? Where did that conception come from? Is it *working*, for both you and your organization? These are tough questions—but they are ones that you have to be willing to ask yourself and, depending on the answers, act on. You can learn, adapt, and change.

Do You Have Faith That Justice Will Prevail?

I believe that in order to succeed as a leader in an organization, you need to, first, have a certain amount of confidence in yourself—in the sense that you believe that you bring unique and valuable talents to your organization, and that the organization is fortunate to have access to those talents.

You also need something more. You need the ability to combine your self-confidence with the ability to make a "leap of faith." In order to develop your own style, pursue your passions, and improve your skills, you have to believe that you are part of a system that recognizes your unique attributes and ultimately rewards your efforts. You have to believe that justice will prevail.

This may seem obvious, but to many young professionals and senior executives I talk with, it isn't. Over the past twenty years, I have seen quite a few leaders at all levels—including more senior executives—underperform against their potential, either because they lacked basic confidence in themselves, or because they didn't believe that the system in which they operated would treat them fairly. As a result, their behaviors often sabotaged their upward progress, personal development, and, ultimately, their contributions to their organizations.

Symptomatic of this lack of faith was a belief, for example, that every action they took should be based on an expectation of what they might receive in return. Would they receive credit, would they get paid, would it help their promotion, would it make them look good to the right people? All these questions were at the forefront of their minds. As a result, they weren't inclined to do things for others without regard to what was "in it for them."

The Need to Believe in Fairness

In several cases, I have personally worked with young professionals as well as more senior leaders who exhibited this type of cynical attitude regarding "fairness" within the corporate context (or the political context, or the nonprofit context). Why did they have this attitude? At one point or another in the course of their careers, they had been "victims" of a perceived injustice. They didn't get the promotion they wanted, or they were denied the compensation they thought they deserved. Maybe they outright failed at a job and concluded that they didn't get a "fair shake." Whatever the specifics, these experiences had a traumatic and lasting impact on their faith in being treated fairly. They developed a belief that justice was unlikely to prevail in the work setting—and that they should conduct themselves accordingly.

If you run your own firm, you may not think that this is a particular problem for you. After all, you are the boss. To my surprise, even in these situations, I have encountered CEOs who feel they have to answer to parents, blood relatives, spouses, siblings, or even their children—and have lost some faith about whether they are, or will be, appreciated for their unique style, skills, and contributions. This is one reason why there are so many "family counselors" who advise small, independent, and family-owned businesses. In these companies, dysfunction and distrust can be just as much a problem as in a large corporation. When I am consulted by CEOs of these firms, their issues often revolve around a loss of confidence in the "system" actually working in ways that they perceive to be fair.

Why does all of this matter? Who cares whether the leader is cynical, or lacks faith in the system? I argue that it matters a *great deal*, because the cynical, disaffected leader finds it very difficult to do the kinds of things that I'm advocating in this book. Rather than focusing on strengths, weaknesses, passions, leadership style improvements, and authenticity, they are often distracted with trying to please someone else. They can't seem to get to an authentic leadership style—or even take that challenge seriously. Invariably, *this has a powerful ripple effect*. If leaders don't believe in fairness of the system, it becomes a self-fulfilling prophecy. They soon find that it is more difficult to create a spirit of teamwork, and to mobilize their troops to work for the good of the company. They find that they have unwittingly encouraged selfish behavior that doesn't serve the interests of either the organization or its clients.

The converse is also true. Creating a system of fairness and meritocracy can be a superb competitive advantage for an organization. Outstanding people gravitate to leaders who are authentic, and to companies in which justice prevails and people are encouraged to reach their true potential based on their own distinctive qualities.

Maybe this strikes you as a little too touchy-feely, or as a little too much ivory-tower baloney. If so, I'd encourage you to think again. There are numerous examples of once great companies that have declined over a period of years based on the erosion of a meritocracy. I have interacted with several of these companies, and I can tell you that one central aspect of their deterioration has been a loss of faith in the leadership and in the company's system of justice. This loss of faith undermined the ability of its executives to perform many of the key leadership tasks described in this book—creating a vision with priorities that mobilizes the troops; coaching, mentoring, and talent development; and creating and maintaining alignment.

In *every* organization, people at all levels have a strong need to believe. They want and need to believe in themselves in order to perform at their best. They want—and ultimately *need*—to believe in their organizations in order to excel. Does your leadership help create this type of environment?

Getting Off Track: The Cynic in Chief

The chief executive of a major professional services company was extremely frustrated with his inability to take his company to the next level of its development. I had known this person for the previous twenty years, and when I joined the faculty at Harvard, he asked whether I would be willing to advise him.

When I first sat down with him, he described his desire to build his company globally and, on the basis of its distinctive competencies, build out key market adjacencies with the company's existing product lines. This strategy made enormous sense to me, and he seemed to be on the right track, so I asked him why he wanted my advice.

He explained that in order to execute this strategy, he would need to move key leaders into several new jobs both domestically and overseas. Unfortunately, he couldn't convince any of the company's key talent to make these moves. As a result, he made several external hires, but many of these new recruits washed out, either because they couldn't adapt to the company's culture, or because they couldn't perform at a sufficiently high level. While the company was struggling to make the necessary personnel moves to implement this new strategy, its competitors were making fast progress and passing the firm in building these businesses. The impact was a loss of market share and increasing strategic vulnerability.

He asked whether I would be willing to help him figure out how to break through this logjam. He encouraged me to talk with a half dozen of his top lieutenants, and offered to make available any key financial or strategic information that I might find useful.

I looked through a wide variety of internal information and then sat down with the six key divisional leaders. I found the discussions with these executives pretty jarring. They explained that "in this company, you get rewarded for generating revenues and profits—*period*." They reported, unapologetically, that not only could they not convince their key employees to change jobs for the good of the company, but they themselves would not want to make personal sacrifices, or take risks with their careers, to advance new company initiatives. They were quite convinced that these types of sacrifices were unlikely to be rewarded. They had seen these initiatives play out in the past, and the executives who took risks wound up damaging their careers.

I asked them to reconcile this attitude with the strategic objectives of the CEO—their boss! They each explained that they had worked closely with the CEO, over many years, during his ascent in the company. They said that he had gotten the chief executive job because his businesses generated substantial revenue, he was good at making sure he got "credit" for what he did, and he was notorious for looking out for his own interests first and foremost. In the past, he had openly expressed cynicism about the kinds of strategic "investment" projects that he was now implementing, and he had discouraged talented executives from taking risks to support them.

In effect, over a period of years, this CEO had created a company of cynics who shared and mirrored his attitudes. He and his cohort of "disbelievers" became more and more successful and gradually took over the company. Now they were being called on to think first about doing things *for the good of the company*: moving overseas, changing jobs, integrating new lateral hires, coaching promising young talent, and so on. They were being asked to make sacrifices and to do things for others that might not clearly help them personally but would help the organization enormously.

This new CEO couldn't get people to do what needed to be done. As a result, as the world changed, the company was veering out of alignment. It became more vulnerable in the marketplace. Competitors started to pass the company by.

The CEO and I had a follow-up meeting in his office. I explained to him what I had discovered: that his key people had learned—*from him!*—that they had to look out for themselves. They had learned that it's dumb (or dangerous) to trust the company, and that it's smart to cover your own behind. They had learned that *this was just a job*. If a seemingly better job came along, they should consider it seriously. They should not "go the extra mile" on the assumption that everyone would benefit from a stronger company. Looking out for number one was the prime directive.

At this point, we agreed to go have dinner—at a location far from his office. During our meal, I asked this CEO to explain to me why he had a reputation within the company for such deep skepticism. He told me two stories about negative experiences he had had earlier in his career—experiences that had shaped his attitude toward his job early on. He related these stories with some passion, indicating that they still rankled. I pointed out that these same experiences happen to lots of professionals during their careers, and that most people manage to shrug them off and move forward. Evidently, he hadn't been able to do that.

He agreed, reluctantly, that his cynical attitude had finally caught up with his ability to successfully perform in his job. The question was: *what to do now?* He decided that he needed to do some serious soul-searching about the underlying assumptions that defined his leadership style. He needed to think hard about justice, and fairness. Was he truly committed to making sure that justice prevailed at the company he now headed? He realized that he didn't have the luxury of being "cynic in chief"; in fact, he had to create a context in which people could believe in the greater good, and in which they would be willing to put the interests of the company—and their colleagues— ahead of their own.

We discussed specific steps he could take to address this situation. First, he would need to start paying and promoting executives based on criteria beyond revenue production—unheard of, in this company. Second, over time, he would need to fill key executive positions with leaders who were willing to make sacrifices on behalf of the company. In order to do these things, he would need to fundamentally change his own definition of a successful executive and be willing to "walk the talk."

I would like to report that this story had a happy ending— but the fact is, in this case, the jury is still out. It is very difficult for human beings to go overnight from being selfish and cynical to doing things first for others, without regard to what's in it for them. This CEO is struggling to change his mind-set and behavior, attempting to create a broader definition of fairness, and working to financially reward and promote leaders based on their broad leadership actions on behalf of the firm, beyond just production.

Do You Instill or Undermine Faith in the Organization?

Are you "cynic in chief"? Are you tearing things down at the same time that you're trying to build them up? If so, you may be building the very thing—a cold and unsupportive work environment—that ultimately undermines leaders and weakens organizations!

Successful organizations are built, in part, on faith. They are built on the faith that if you do the right thing, be yourself, help others, and sacrifice for the enterprise, then justice will prevail. No, that doesn't mean that there won't be injustice in specific situations, or that things won't ever be out of "karmic balance"—for sure, they will be!—but over the long run, justice will prevail.

Do you have this faith? Have you created it among your people?

Let's assume that you are resolved to do a better job at this. How do you do it? First, *watch your own rhetoric*. People will listen to every word that you say, as their leader. Be careful about the offhand comment—it may come back to bite you.

Second, *reward employees for more than just commercial production*. Reward the behaviors you want to reinforce—coaching, taking on tough assignments, recruiting, superb client service, relationship building, and being brave enough to turn down business that could tarnish the reputation of the firm. In other words, reinforce the behaviors that *build a great firm* as well as fuel a commercial engine.

The Courage to Speak Up!

Let's take on one more important issue in this chapter, which has to do with the positive consequences of being yourself in a "fair" workplace.

One of the byproducts of an environment in which people are convinced that justice will generally prevail is that they become much more willing to speak up, express their opinions, and disagree when appropriate. Great organizations are based on people being willing to behave in this way. I would argue that if you're fortunate enough to work at a place like this, you have a positive obligation to make it your job to decide what you believe, and then express it or act on it.

How many times have you sat in a meeting in which someone authoritative is making an argument, and you have no idea what they are talking about? Is everyone around the table nodding knowingly—as if they understand and agree with what is being said? Influenced by this peer pressure, perhaps you decide that you should nod, too, even though you still don't have the foggiest notion of what is going on. After the presentation, everyone around the table effuses about that authoritative person. You might even join in with your own praise: *nice job!*

But what if *no one* around the table really understood, much less agreed with, what was being said? What if they all felt peer pressure to pretend they did? What if no one had the confidence and the courage to raise his or her hand and admit, "I'm sorry, but I don't understand what you're saying; and, of what I *do* understand, I don't think I agree"?

When everybody nods even when they don't actually agree, terrible decisions can be made, and major mistakes can happen. No one around the table feels confident or accountable enough to disagree with the boss or their peers—or even, in some cases, their subordinates. They don't have enough faith in their own views. They worry that maybe they're just dumber than everyone else, or maybe they're just slow that morning—when in fact, they are as sharp as anyone around the table, and their disagreement would be welcomed by their colleagues and would be likely to lead to a much better debate and discussion.

Have you ever observed something like this? Worse, have you been a willing participant?

The Essence of Leadership

Over my five years of teaching at Harvard, students ranging from young MBAs to visiting executives have asked me for my definition of the term *leadership*. Does it mean commanding others? Does it mean you are charismatic or able to give a compelling speech? Does it mean simply that, for whatever reason, people want to follow you? Are you born with it, or is it something that you learn?

My definition of leadership is as follows: *a leader works hard to figure out what he or she believes, and then has the courage to act on it.* Yes, there are many attributes of a leader, but at the core, this is what a leader must do. According to this definition, it's not about the size of your empire or the specifics of your job description. A person can be a leader even without having any direct reports or any formal assigned responsibilities.

By this definition, exhibiting strong leadership can be as simple as being willing to speak up and express your views. According to this definition, are you a leader? Do you develop leadership in your organization by encouraging people to express their views? Do you promote and reward leadership behavior?

Many people are drawn to the superficial aspects of leadership—trappings such as title, significant management responsibilities, and money—but they fail to meet the fundamental test of leadership: working hard to figure out what they believe, and then having the courage to *act* on those beliefs. This failure often explains the cases in which organizations get off track and drift into trouble. Even though their executives, young and old, may disagree with a number of existing practices, they are hesitant to raise these issues, challenge their superiors, develop and suggest alternative solutions, and generally *assert* themselves.

An Intimidating Leadership Style: The Tap That Feels Like a Hammer

An extremely successful private company was led by a very talented CEO who had a very confrontational and argumentative leadership style. I know this CEO well, and the truth is that he actually welcomes disagreement—a good thing—but his style is sufficiently caustic that he often intimidates people, and sometimes unintentionally discourages them from expressing their opinions. If you engage in a debate with him, you'd better have your facts lined up, because he is going to aggressively challenge you and even criticize you personally—and that is likely to make you feel quite defensive or even stupid.

As a result of his style, many of his senior leaders adopted what they believed was a sensible strategy, as described to me by one of his senior lieutenants: "Try to figure out what the CEO thinks, and make an effort to express that view when speaking to him. If you can express this view before he does, that's even better—because he'll think that you are of like minds, and he'll think more highly of you!"

Despite this leadership style, the company performed quite well for many years, and the CEO had a good reputation as a strong manager and leader. Then came the economic crisis that began in 2007, and the downside of the company's leadership culture started to become evident.

The CEO had made certain decisions that damaged the company's carefully cultivated franchise. In the decision-making process, several top executives had apprehensions but decided to bite their tongues and stay silent. One or two spoke out, expressing muted concerns, but buckled quickly when the CEO actively challenged their arguments. Still others dealt with their concerns by deciding it was a good time to leave the company.

The CEO called me in late 2008 and asked that I help him deal with some of the damage the company had suffered in the previous two years. We first did a diagnosis of the company's current franchise and dissected certain key decisions that had been made during this period. He gave me free rein to talk to several of his top lieutenants.

In my discussions, I heard about apprehension regarding several critical decisions that had been made. I learned about the CEO's leadership style and the lack of debate and disagreement. Upon hearing some of this, the CEO made it clear to me that he was quite annoyed that at least some of his key leaders did not have the courage to stand up and disagree at the time these decisions were being made.

I agreed to lead an off-site with the CEO and his top ten leaders. We set this up as a no-holds-barred discussion, where everyone needed to come prepared to speak their minds—except the CEO, who was required to remain silent and listen. Over the course of several hours, the CEO listened, and learned. He came to realize that he had unintentionally destroyed one of the company's natural potential strengths: a strong senior leadership team that debated, disagreed, and, as a consequence, made good decisions. For their part, his executives came to realize that they had become too intimidated by the boss's argumentative style, and they needed to speak up forcefully and frequently.

Since this off-site, the company has been able to repair much of the damage that was done to the business. More important, it has created a new and better dynamic that requires the CEO to encourage dissent, and also requires junior as well as senior leaders to take responsibility for speaking up.

The Risks of Playing It Too Safe: Getting to the Right Mind-Set

Over the years, I have seen terrible damage done to companies in which talented emerging as well as senior leaders stayed quiet or played it safe as described in the anecdote above.

What's the remedy? I like to advise people to *play the game with a degree of abandon.*

What does this mean? Use your best judgment regarding your tone and your timing—but have the confidence to *say what you think.* You have that obligation to your company and to your colleagues. Speak up when you don't understand, and especially when you don't agree. Great companies are built around a willingness to debate and disagree, and on the wise decisions that arise out of those disagreements. People in these companies are true to themselves, and act like owners.

Many of the suggestions in this chapter are about a mind-set. It is fair to say that cultivating this mind-set is easier said than done, especially if you have a mortgage, car payments, college tuitions, and weddings to pay for, and all the other obligations of "successful" people in today's world.

"Thanks for the advice," I can hear some readers saying. "I'll make sure to follow it someday when I have more money and more career security."

My response would be that following these suggestions *now*, especially as a young professional, will help you create the type of security you're seeking and the success you desire. More important, these suggestions will help you get the most out of your talents and reach your unique potential.

There are also some personal habits that, if adopted, may make it easier for you to cultivate the right mind-set. You've seen these comments in earlier chapters, but they are worth repeating here. First, my *strong* advice to every person I advise, young and old, is to *save your money.* One business school professor has described this as "walk-away money" or—less politely—"go-to-hell money." Whatever you want to call it, I think it is wise to put yourself in a position to love your job, but avoid being *in* love with your job. You don't want to be a slave to your job to the extent that you're insecure and afraid to take some risks.

This is also why it pays to take an appropriate amount of vacation, eat a proper diet, exercise, cultivate hobbies outside work, and generally do things that give you some perspective and emotional distance at work. By cultivating your own emotional independence, you make yourself more valuable to your organization.

Last, and most important, remember that the point of the game is to reach *your* potential—not someone else's. If you are true to yourself and your values, and you work on being the best you can be, you're far more likely to feel like a big success in the future—whatever your ultimate accomplishments.

Suggested Follow-up Steps

1. Make a list of your three greatest strengths and your three greatest weaknesses. Get advice from your senior, peer, and junior coaches or advisers in order to make sure your list reflects "reality" in relation to your current job and aspirations.

2. Develop a specific action plan to work on your weaknesses. Action steps might include specific job assignments, seeking feedback within your organization, and/or getting an outside coach.

3. Encourage your subordinates to do this same analysis and action planning. Discuss these plans in your coaching sessions for subordinates.

4. Think of a situation in which you were at your best, when you performed extremely well and felt great about your impact. What were the elements of this situation? What tasks were you performing, what was your leadership approach, what was the context, and what other factors enhanced your performance? What lessons do you take from this, regarding your passions, values, and other key elements that help bring out your best performance?

5. Think of a time when you brought out the best in others. What was your motivational approach? What was your leadership style? What other elements allowed you to bring out the best in others? When you reflect on this situation, what lessons do you learn about yourself, including about your philosophy and values, as well as how you might best motivate others in the future?

8

Bringing It All Together

The Practice of Gaining Perspective

The Great Recession and its aftermath have affected different regions, industries, and companies in a variety of ways. Leaders globally have spent the past several years working hard to adapt to new realities and pursue new opportunities. These same leaders are also working to assess their current competitive positioning and organizational competencies, evaluate and improve their leadership effectiveness, develop ideas for what they need to do now, and formulate specific strategies for implementing those ideas.

Over the past number of years and in various contexts, I have observed and worked closely with a number of emerging as well as senior leaders—helping them to assess, restructure, grow, develop, and effectively build their enterprises. I have drawn on my own leadership experiences (which include making more than a few mistakes). I have had the opportunity to learn from a wide variety of leaders regarding those practices that have helped them become substantially more effective. Based on these experiences, which ranged across a wide spectrum of issues, industries, continents, and personalities, I decided to write this book.

My objective has been to share lessons I have learned regarding how to be a more successful leader and how to develop other effective leaders within an organization. As we have discussed, this effort starts with developing specific habits and processes that foster sustainable success.

Reflection: Allocating Time and Resources to Addressing the Big Questions

Leading an organization can be very demanding, and even chaotic. As a result, not surprisingly, many leaders struggle to find time to reflect on important issues. When they finally do, it sometimes occurs too late for them to anticipate competitive threats, seize attractive opportunities, or make critical changes that would help advance their organizations—and their own careers.

The primary objective of this book is *not* to suggest specific steps you should take to build your career or your organization. I certainly wouldn't presume to try to give you that kind of advice. Every person and organization is unique. Each industry, geographic, and cultural context has a profound impact on what approaches and strategies make sense in a particular situation. Instead, the primary objective of this book is to encourage you to reflect on and consider "what to ask the person in the mirror."

In the preceding chapters, I have challenged you to call "time-out," so that you can step back and *ask certain key questions*. Time-out doesn't mean stopping your activities—instead, it means consciously allocating the time and other resources necessary to address big questions.

I have suggested when, why, and how to frame the questions that you should be asking yourself and your organization. These questions are intended to get at critical issues that you should be attempting to frame and address. I have described numerous actual examples of this framing process, as well as obstacles that arise, and suggested how you might address these questions based on your specific circumstances.

Many of these issues and questions will be thought-provoking and will require a good bit of further questioning, analysis, and reflection. Most likely, you won't be able to answer them by yourself. They will require the help and insight of your employees and potentially other external resources.

You Don't Need to Have All the Answers

Fortunately, the key to managing and leading your organization and your career does *not* lie in "having all the answers." The key lies in making a conscious effort to regularly step back to reflect, and then identify and frame the issues that are central to leading your organization effectively into the future.

I believe that asking the right questions is usually 90 percent of the battle. If this sounds obvious to you, ask yourself how regularly you actually do it. In fact, most executives go through this exercise *far less frequently* than they should. It's understandable, because all too often, they get caught up in the pressing issues of the day. Typically, there's almost always something more urgent to attend to. Also, many executives' first instinct is to come up with an *answer*, rather than to ask a question. Finally, many executives struggle to turn their specific concerns into well-framed questions that can be productively studied and debated. Unfortunately, delaying or avoiding this type of inquiry can cause you to get severely sidetracked.

The Inquiry Habit

Proactive and regular inquiry is healthy, is habit forming, and will keep your career and organization on the right track. In my experience, outstanding executives tend to pursue this approach and build this discipline into their best leadership practices. They find that the more they practice insightful inquiry and reflection, the more effective they become in using it as a powerful tool.

Established leaders as well as young professionals can benefit from adopting these practices. The sooner in your career you begin to develop these habits, the better. It's a little bit like strenuous physical activity on a regular basis: it doesn't sound like fun, and may not sound as important as the fifty other things you have to fit into your day—but it *works*.

Let's assume that after reading the previous chapters, you're convinced, and you're eager to build a tailored version of these questions and practices into your organization and into your leadership style. How do you go about doing it? I would make two primary suggestions: build time for reflection into your life, and build it into the life of your organization.

Create Space for Reflection in Your Life

I recommend that you consciously structure your time in a manner that, amid the chaos of work and life, creates opportunities for you to step back and reflect. You need to create windows of time in which you can get perspective, and think about key issues from an emotional distance.

Some suggestions I have made to executives on this front include these:

- Take a vacation at least once every three or four months. That's three to four vacations a year. At least two of those vacations should be the kind in which you have substantial slack time, with ample opportunity to think. I'm advocating "lying on the beach" time, as opposed to "eight cities in seven days" time.

- Build identified slack time into your regular schedule. Make sure that you get home for dinner several nights a week. Block out time on the weekends for decompression, reflection, and catching up on your sleep. Plan for and *protect* those time slots from the kinds of tempting incursions that inevitably present themselves. Realize that time spent running around at night and on weekends may be exhilarating, but it's rarely conducive to reflection and perspective.

- Make it a priority to take better care of yourself. Assuming that you don't have physical restrictions, schedule exercise on some regular basis. Watch your diet, and see a doctor regularly. When you feel good physically and get your sleep, your brain will work better, and you'll find it easier to tackle tough issues objectively and with some emotional distance. *Being fresh* is a critical contributor to your ability to reflect.

- Find other ways to create balance in your life. I sounded this theme in previous chapters. By *balance*, I mean engaging in activities that take your mind off your work for sustained periods of time. This may mean time with loved ones, nonprofit work, intellectual pursuits, service in your community, or other activities—activities that can help you put your organization and job in some type of broader context.

These are just a few suggestions, and I'm sure you can think of other actions, suited to you, that serve this larger purpose. *The goal is to carve out some space and room for creating focus and gaining perspective.* You need to position yourself so that you can coherently ask some of the vital questions framed in this book—or your own versions thereof.

What else? I have found it very useful to keep a short list of key questions (including many of those in this book) on the wall of my office. On a regular basis, they remind me of the issues and questions that I don't want to lose sight of. Periodically, I update these questions as my job changes and the world changes. If I find that I'm getting too distracted to think about them, I make a note to myself that I need to schedule time away from the office in order to reflect on one or more of these issues.

You need to figure out and do whatever works for you. However you do it, I urge you to consciously build windows of time in your life to reflect, diagnose, and move forward.

The Reflective Organization

In addition to incorporating this approach into your professional life, you need to bring some of this mind-set into the life of your organization.

Many companies develop processes and events that help create opportunities for the leadership to take time to reflect, frame issues, debate, and move forward with key initiatives. Some leadership groups make good use of these opportunities. Others, unfortunately, don't recognize their value, and wind up going through the motions or squandering them in other ways.

Examples of these opportunities include a Monday morning meeting of senior leadership, monthly or quarterly dinners for senior leaders, leadership off-sites, special task forces to address key issues, and so on. Do you have these types of meetings, events, and task forces scheduled into the life of your company? If so, how do you use them? Do you use them as opportunities to reflect? Or are they more procedural and process oriented—the kinds of interactions in which people merely provide status reports, in which debate and disagreement are subtly discouraged, and issues aren't adequately framed and discussed?

How many times have you heard a leader say that he or she hates meetings? How often have you yourself said that? In my experience, the problem is less with the "meeting" per se and more often a result of the way the meeting is framed and choreographed. A poorly choreographed meeting *is* a waste of time, and the participants have every right to be annoyed by it.

If you *have* scheduled time for a meeting, have you prepared sufficiently to make sure you are using that time wisely? Have you structured the meeting so that important issues are framed and key topics are actively debated? Do you schedule time for *reflection* with your senior leaders?

If you're not happy with your answers to any of these questions, step back and rethink your approach. Most meetings are wasted because the leader rolls in to the meeting relatively unprepared, at least in the ways that I'm advocating. He or she has not thought about the major subjects to be framed, hasn't gotten a sense of the members of the group regarding the burning issues that need to be discussed, and isn't prepared to conduct an effective discussion in which the participants *participate* and gain real insights.

This approach requires preparation and thought, and argues for a "segmentation" of meetings. Keep the procedural and update meetings brief and to the point. (The regular Monday morning meeting can suffice.) Separately, plan for longer debate-and-discussion meetings that are held far less often— preferably away from the office and at a time of day when participants are not looking over their shoulders to worry about events back at the office.

For these meetings, you need to think through issues in advance, be prepared to pose a small number of key questions for discussion, and probably ask the attendees to come prepared to debate and discuss particular issues. These meetings should always have well-understood follow-up, so that great insights aren't lost and good suggestions are actually pursued. When you conduct meetings or off-sites in this manner, your team will be strengthened, your stature will be enhanced, and you will identify actions that, when taken, are likely to strengthen the business.

Make sure you are creating this space for reflection with your team. If you haven't done so, you are missing key opportunities to advance your organization. In addition, more broadly, as you schedule key events in the life of your company, as you retool processes, and as you set priorities, build in that time for reflection. These meetings are an opportunity to reiterate your vision and priorities, and emphasize your values. They create opportunities for you to listen and learn, as you give voice to your people.

Into the Future

These suggestions are intended to help you navigate through your future. The next several years are likely to be a time of immense change. True, we've recently been through a difficult period, but I believe the next several years will test the abilities and adaptability of leaders at least as much.

Fortunately, despite notes of skepticism from naysayers and pessimists, my interactions with thousands of executives from all over the world have convinced me that leadership is alive and well in today's companies and nonprofit organizations. Thousands of leaders are taking the time to seek advice, study best practices, and learn how they can hone and build their leadership and management skills.

I am continually inspired by their example, and by their openness to learning. I am hopeful that at least some of the questions and advice in this book will prove to be useful tools—for you, and for them.

Suggested Follow-up Step

1. Keep the appendix of this book on your wall (or some other convenient spot) and look it over regularly. Ask yourself whether you are taking sufficient time to consider these topics. Are you asking the critical questions that will help you increase the effectiveness of your organization?

Appendix

Critical Questions for Becoming
a More Effective Leader and
Reaching Your Potential

Vision and Priorities

In the press of day-to-day activities, leaders often fail to adequately communicate their vision to the organization, and in particular, they don't communicate it in a way that helps their subordinates determine where to focus their own efforts.

- Have you developed a clear vision for your enterprise?
- Have you identified three to five key priorities to achieve that vision?
- Do you actively communicate this vision, and associated key priorities, to your organization?

Suggested Follow-up Steps

- Write down, in three to four sentences, a clear vision for your enterprise or business unit. (If it's helpful, use the

exercises described in "Developing a Vision: Some Useful Exercises" in chapter 1.)

- List the three to five key priorities that are most critical to achieving this vision. These should be tasks that
  you must do extraordinarily well in order for you to
  succeed based on where you are positioned today.
  (If you are having trouble narrowing them down to
  three to five, use the "1s, 2s, 3s" exercise described in
  chapter 1.)

- Ask yourself whether the vision (with priorities) is
  sufficiently clear and understandable. In addition, ask
  yourself whether you communicate the vision and
  priorities frequently enough that your key stakeholders
  (e.g., direct reports and employees) could repeat them
  back to you. Interview key employees to see whether
  they understand and can clearly rearticulate the vision
  and priorities.

- Identify venues and occasions for the regular
  communication, reiteration, and discussion of the vision
  and priorities. Create opportunities for questions and
  answers.

- Assemble your executive team off-site to debate the
  vision and priorities. In particular, consider whether
  the vision and priorities still fit the competitive environment, changes in the world, and the needs of the business. Use the off-site to update your vision and priorities
  and to ensure buy-in on the part of your senior leadership team.

Managing Your Time

Leaders need to know how they're spending their time. They also need to ensure that their time allocation (and that of their subordinates) matches their key priorities.

- Do you know how you spend your time?
- Does it match your key priorities?

Suggested Follow-up Steps

- Track your time for two weeks and break down the results into major categories.

- Compare how this breakdown matches or is mismatched versus your three to five key priorities. Make a list of the matches and mismatches. Regarding the mismatches, write down those time allocations that are 2s and 3s and could therefore be performed by others—or should not be performed at all.

- Create an action plan for dealing with the mismatches. For example, commit to delegating those tasks that could just as easily be performed by someone else. Decide, in advance, to say no to certain time requests that do not fit your key priorities.

- After a few months, repeat the preceding three steps. Assess whether you are doing a better job of spending your time on critical priorities.

- Encourage your subordinates to perform these same steps.

Giving and Getting Feedback

Leaders often fail to coach employees in a direct and timely fashion and, instead, wait until the year-end review. This approach may lead to unpleasant surprises and can undermine effective professional development. Just as important, leaders need to cultivate subordinates who can give them advice and feedback during the year.

- Do you coach and actively develop your key people?

- Is your feedback specific, timely, and actionable?

- Do you solicit actionable feedback from your key subordinates?

- Do you cultivate advisers who are able to confront you with criticisms that you may not want to hear?

Suggested Follow-up Steps

- For each of your direct reports, write down three to five specific strengths. In addition, write down at least two or three specific skills or tasks that you believe they could improve on in order to improve their performance and advance their careers. Allocate time to directly observing their performance, and discreetly make inquiries to gather information and insights in order to prepare this analysis.

- Schedule time with each subordinate, at least six months in advance of the year-end review, to discuss your observations and identify specific action steps that could help them improve and address their developmental needs and opportunities.

- Write down a realistic list of your own strengths and weaknesses. Make a list of at least five subordinates from whom you could solicit feedback regarding your strengths and weaknesses. Meet with each subordinate individually and explain that you need their help. In your meetings, make sure to ask them to give you advice regarding at least one or two tasks or skills they believe you could improve on. Thank them for their help.

- Write down an action plan for addressing your own weaknesses and developmental needs. If you have a direct superior (or trusted peer), consider soliciting advice regarding your developmental needs and potential action steps. Depending on your situation and level in the organization, consider the option of hiring an outside coach.

- Encourage each of your direct reports to follow these same steps regarding their direct reports and themselves.

Succession Planning and Delegation

When leaders fail to actively plan for succession, they do not delegate sufficiently and may become decision-making bottlenecks. Key employees may leave if they are not actively groomed and challenged.

- Do you have a succession-planning process for key positions?

- Have you identified potential successors for your job?

- If not, what is stopping you?

- Do you delegate sufficiently?
- Have you become a decision-making bottleneck?

Suggested Follow-up Steps

- Create a succession-planning depth chart for your business unit or organization (as described in chapter 4). This document should include at least two or three potential successors for your own position.

- For each potential successor, write down their key development needs and specific actions you might take in order to develop their capabilities in relation to potential future positions. Work to develop and shape these specific development plans. Make use of the developmental action plans prepared as part of your chapter 3 follow-up steps.

- For those key tasks that you have committed to finding a way to delegate (see chapter 2), begin matching those tasks with specific candidates on the depth chart. Make assignments.

- Categorize delegated tasks in terms of their levels of importance to your enterprise. Based on this analysis, note which tasks need to be done at extremely high levels of quality, and which can be done at "sufficient" levels of quality. Ask whether you have calibrated your level of involvement to this categorization, and remember that "involvement" should often take the form of coaching the subordinate, rather than a direct intervention. Make a commitment to "picking your spots," to ensure that your direct interventions (beyond coaching) are justified by an appropriately high level of task importance.

- Ask your business unit leaders to perform this same exercise with regard to their direct reports.

Evaluation and Alignment

The world is constantly changing, and leaders need to be able to adapt their businesses accordingly.

- Is the design of your company still aligned with your vision and priorities?
- If you had to design the enterprise today with a clean sheet of paper, how would you change the people, key tasks, organizational structure, culture, and your leadership style?
- Why haven't you made these changes?
- Have you pushed yourself and your organization to do this clean-sheet-of-paper exercise?

Suggested Follow-up Steps

- Identify a key business unit or function to try out the clean-sheet-of-paper exercise. Create a small task force based on the selected names from the succession-planning depth chart exercise. Attempt to draw professionals from at least two to three different business units and/or functional areas. Give the team a specific assignment, and emphasize that they should assume that there are no sacred cows to be protected. Make clear to them that while you may not follow every piece of their advice, you want their candid views and most likely will implement at least some of their suggestions.

- Agree on an appropriate time frame. Take into account that this assignment is not in place of doing their day jobs. Make clear that you are available to answer questions or give guidance, but you plan to stay away from this process in order to avoid influencing their analysis and conclusions.

- Debrief the group regarding their findings. Also, conduct a post mortem to determine what you and the task force learned from the process of doing this exercise.

- Develop a specific action plan for implementing at least some (if not all) of the group's recommendations.

The Leader as Role Model

Your actions are closely observed by those around you. They send a powerful message about what you believe and what you truly value.

- Do you act as a role model?
- Do your behaviors match your words?
- How do you conduct yourself under pressure?
- Is your conduct consistent with your stated values?

Suggested Follow-up Steps

- Write down two or three key messages you believe you send with your behavior (versus your speeches). Seek advice from key subordinates and advisers who directly observe your behavior, in order to answer this question: is there a disconnect between the messages you wish to send and those you are in fact sending?

- Do this same exercise for your key direct reports. What messages is each of them sending about what is truly valued in your organization? Again, make discreet inquiries, if necessary, to do this analysis. Incorporate this work into your coaching of these executives.

- Think of a situation in which you felt enormous stress at work and regretted your behavior. Write down the one or two issues that created the stress you were feeling—acknowledging that these issues may have had nothing to do with work. How would you behave differently if you could replay this situation? Write down one or two lessons you take away from this exercise.

Reaching Your Potential

Successful executives develop leadership styles that fit the needs of their business but also fit their own beliefs and personality.

- Are you pursuing a path that is consistent with your assessment of your strengths, weaknesses, and passions?

- If not, what are you waiting for?

- Have you developed your own style at work?

- Do you speak up, express your opinions, and conduct yourself with confidence?

- Do you encourage your people to be authentic and express their opinions?

Suggested Follow-up Steps

- Make a list of your three greatest strengths and your three greatest weaknesses. Get advice from your senior, peer, and junior coaches or advisers in order to make sure your list reflects "reality" in relation to your current job and aspirations.

- Develop a specific action plan to work on your weaknesses. Action steps might include specific job assignments, seeking feedback within your organization, and/or getting an outside coach.

- Encourage your subordinates to do this same analysis and action planning. Discuss these plans in your coaching sessions for subordinates.

- Think of a situation in which you were at your best, when you performed extremely well and felt great about your impact. What were the elements of this situation? What tasks were you performing, what was your leadership approach, what was the context, and what other factors enhanced your performance? What lessons do you take from this, regarding your passions, values, and other key elements that help bring out your best performance?

- Think of a time when you brought out the best in others. What was your motivational approach? What was your leadership style? What other elements allowed you to bring out the best in others? When you reflect on this situation, what lessons do you learn about yourself, including about your philosophy and values, as well as how you might best motivate others in the future?

What to Ask the Person in the Mirror: A Framework

Strategic direction and key choices

Vision and priorities
If you know where you're going, it's a lot easier to get there (Chapter 1)

Critical leadership processes

Managing your time
How you spend your time should flow directly from your vision and key priorities (Chapter 2)

Giving and getting feedback
Effective leaders coach their people and actively seek coaching themselves (Chapter 3)

Succession planning and delegation
Owning the challenge of developing successors in your organization (Chapter 4)

Evaluation and alignment
The courage to assess your enterprise with a clean sheet of paper (Chapter 5)

Becoming a leader

The leader as role model
Communicating what you truly believe and value (Chapter 6)

Reaching your potential
Being true to yourself (Chapter 7)

Developing a process for inquiry and reflection

Bringing it all together
The practice of gaining perspective (Chapter 8)

Ask the critical questions

Create space for reflection and debate

Pursue follow-up steps

Potential outcomes

- Greater insight
- Enhanced perspective
- Improved judgment
- Better decisions
- Further inquiry

Notes and Additional References

Chapter 1

1. See James C. Collins and Jerry I. Porras, "Building Your Company's Vision," *Harvard Business Review*, September–October 1996, 65–77; and John P. Kotter, "What Leaders Really Do," *Harvard Business Review*, December 2001, 85–97.

2. Martin Luther King, Jr., "I Have a Dream," August 28, 1963, Washington, D.C.

3. Robert Steven Kaplan, Christopher Marquis, and Brent Kazan, "The Miami Project to Cure Paralysis," Case 9-408-003 (Boston: Harvard Business School, 2008).

4. Barack Obama, keynote address, Democratic National Convention, Boston, MA, July 27, 2004.

5. See http://www.teakfellowship.org/.

6. See http://www.ifoapplestore.com/the_stores.html.

7. See http://www.ge.com/company/culture/leadership_learning.html.

8. Robert Steven Kaplan and Sophie Hood, "Bob Beall at the Cystic Fibrosis Foundation," Case 9–409-107 (Boston: Harvard Business School, 2009).

Chapter 2

1. Stephen R. Covey, *The Seven Habits of Highly Effective People: Restoring the Character Ethic* (New York: Simon and Schuster, 1989).

Chapter 3

1. See John J. Gabarro and Linda A. Hill, "Managing Performance," Case 9-496-022 (Boston: Harvard Business School, 2002); Leslie A. Perlow, Scott A. Snook, and Brian J. Delacey, "Coach Knight: The Will to Win," Case 9-405-041 (Boston: Harvard Business School, 2005); and Leslie A. Perlow, Scott A. Snook, and Brian J. Delacey, "Coach K: Matter of the Heart," Case 9-406-044 (Boston: Harvard Business School, 2005).

Chapter 4

1. Doris Kearns Goodwin, *Team of Rivals: The Political Genius of Abraham Lincoln* (New York: Simon & Schuster, 2005).

2. Linda A. Hill and Maria T. Farkas, "Note on Building and Leading Your Senior Team," Case 9-402-037 (Boston: Harvard Business School, 2002).

Chapter 5

1. See Michael L. Tushman and David A. Nadler, *Competing by Design: The Power of Organizational Architectures* (New York: Oxford University Press, 1997). See also Linda A. Hill, "Note for Analyzing Work Groups," Case 9-496-026 (Boston: Harvard Business School, 1998); and Michael L. Tushman and Charles A. O'Reilly III, "Managerial Problem Solving: A Congruence Approach," 2430BC (Boston: Harvard Business School Press, 2007).

2. William W. George and Andrew N. McLean, "Anne Mulcahy: Leading Xerox Through the Perfect Storm," Case 9-405-050 (Boston: Harvard Business School, 2005); see also "Xerox Corporation: Anne Mulcahy, Chairman & CEO, Leadership & Corporate Accountability class," video, product numbers 9-408-714 (DVD) and 9-408-715 (VHS) (Boston: Harvard Business School, 2008).

Chapter 6

See Linda A. Hill, "Becoming the Boss," *Harvard Business Review*, January 2007, 48–56.

Chapter 7

1. Laura Morgan Roberts, Gretchen Spreitzer, Jane Dutton, Robert Quinn, Emily Heaphy, and Brianna Barker, "How to Play to Your Strengths," *Harvard Business Review*, January 2005, 74–80.

2. Leslie A. Perlow and Scott A. Snook, "Coach Knight: The Will to Win and Coach K: A Matter of the Heart," Case Teaching Note 9-406-103 (Boston: Harvard Business School, 2007).

See also Warren G. Bennis and Robert J. Thomas, "Crucibles of Leadership," *Harvard Business Review*, September 2002, 39–45; William W. George, *True North: Discover Your Authentic Leadership* (San Francisco: Jossey-Bass, 2007); Daniel Goleman, "What Makes a Leader?," *Harvard Business Review*, January 2004, 82–91; and Roderick M. Kramer, "The Harder They Fall," *Harvard Business Review*, October 2003, 58–66.

Acknowledgments

The ideas and concepts in this book are drawn from a variety of experiences over the past several decades.

I owe a great deal to the numerous mentors, coaches, friends, colleagues, clients, and students whom I have had the privilege to know over these many years. Their wisdom—as well as generosity in sharing their stories and challenges—has been critical to all that I have learned and forms the basis for much of this book.

I had the good fortune to start my career at Goldman Sachs. The firm and its leaders helped me to develop a business philosophy and approach that I was able to test in a variety of leadership positions over twenty-two years. The firm's superb clients were generous with their time, wisdom, and ideas—well beyond the requirements of professional relationships. Several of the firm's senior leaders, as well as a significant number of clients, served as critical role models in helping me develop my management abilities and leadership skills.

I am enormously grateful to my colleagues at Harvard Business School. They gave me the opportunity to join the faculty in 2005 and have always helped me to become a more effective professor—coaching me to better frame issues, orchestrate effective discussions, and expand my techniques for helping leaders improve their performance. My fellow professors are enormously generous and rigorous thinkers, intensely interested in the real world and how to improve it. That's a potent combination, and one that has motivated me to further develop my skills and keep learning. I particularly want to thank Nitin Nohria, Bill George, Boris Groysberg, Ranjay Gulati, and Chris Marquis for reviewing the manuscript for this book and giving me excellent feedback.

My classroom experiences have been hugely influential in shaping this book. Since coming to Harvard, I have had the opportunity to teach a substantial number of MBAs and executives at all levels, which has given me exposure to a wide array of leadership, strategy, and competitive challenges. My executive interactions have taught me a great deal about leadership and provided a great laboratory for experimenting with various approaches for improving performance.

I want to thank the *Harvard Business Review* for giving me the opportunity to write articles on leadership and individual development potential. Jeff Kehoe and his colleagues at the Harvard Business Review Press—including Erin Brown, Courtney Cashman, Ellen Peebles, and Allison Peter—encouraged me to use those articles as a basis for saying more and worked with me at every step to create this book.

I could not have written this book without the help of my editor, Jeff Cruikshank. Jeff is an accomplished author in his own right and served as a superb coach, mentor, and editor.

I also want to thank Sandy Martin, my fabulous long-time assistant, who puts up with me and makes it possible for me to function efficiently and effectively. Jane Barrett, my assistant at HBS, has been invaluable and outstanding in all that she does. Both have helped to keep this project on track over the past two years.

Special thanks to Karen Belgiovine, Michael Diamond, Heather Henriksen, Colleen Kaftan, Arlene Kagan, Scott Richardson, Wendy Winer, and David Winer for reading and advising me on various portions of this manuscript.

Last and most important, I want to thank my parents and family. They have given me love, support, and understanding at every point in my life. Their philosophy, values, and advice echo in the pages of this book.

Index

About the Author

Robert Steven Kaplan is a professor of management practice at Harvard Business School and co-chairman of Draper Richards Kaplan Foundation, a global venture philanthropy firm.

Prior to joining Harvard in 2005, he served as vice-chairman of the Goldman Sachs Group, Inc., with global oversight responsibility for the Investment Banking and Investment Management divisions. He was a member of the firm's Management Committee and co-chairman of its Partnership Committee, and chaired the firm's Pine Street leadership program for developing emerging leaders. He previously served as global co-head of the Investment Banking division, head of the Corporate Finance department, and head of Asia-Pacific Investment Banking (headquartered in Tokyo, Japan). He became a partner of the firm in 1990.

Throughout his career, Kaplan has worked extensively with nonprofit and community organizations. He is the founding co-chairman of the Harvard NeuroDiscovery Center Advisory Board, co-chairman of Project ALS, and founding co-chairman of the TEAK Fellowship. He also is co-chairman of the Executive Committee for Harvard University's Office for Sustainability, as well as a member of the boards of Harvard Medical School and Harvard Management Company (serving as interim president and chief executive officer from November 2007 to June 2008).

Previously, Kaplan was appointed by the governor of Kansas to serve as a member of the Kansas Healthcare Policy Authority Board. He also served as a member of the Capital Markets Advisory Group for the New York Federal Reserve.

Kaplan is a member of the board of the State Street Corporation, chairman of the Investment Advisory committee of Google Inc., a senior adviser to Indaba Capital Management LLC, and an advisory director of Berkshire Partners LLC. He previously served on the board of Bed, Bath and Beyond, Inc. (1994–2009). He serves in an advisory capacity to a number of other companies and organizations. Over the course of his career, Kaplan has advised and worked closely with senior executives in both the for-profit and the not-for-profit sectors. He has also coached an extensive variety of professionals in the early and middle stages of their careers.

As a professor of management practice at Harvard Business School, Kaplan has taught a variety of leadership courses in the school's MBA program and has also taught a substantial number of experienced leaders in the Harvard Business School executive education programs. He is the author of a number of Harvard Business School cases regarding leadership and has written two highly regarded *Harvard Business Review* articles: "What to Ask the Person in the Mirror" and "Reaching Your Potential."

Kaplan grew up in Prairie Village, Kansas, and received his BS from the University of Kansas. He received his MBA from Harvard Business School, where he was a Baker Scholar.